Hollywood 101

THE ULTIMATE COMMERCIAL BOOK
for kids and Teens

"The Young Actors' Commercial Study-guide!"

by

Chambers Stevens

SANDCASTLE
PUBLISHING &
DISTRIBUTION
south pasadena, california

The Ultimate Commercial Books for Kids & Teens!

The Young Actors' Commercial Study-guide!

Copyright © 2005 by Chambers Stevens

Book Cover & Interior Design by Renee Rolle-Whatley

Book Cover Photography by Nathan Hope

The images used herein were obtained from IMSI's Master Clips©/MasterPhotos© Collection, 1895 Francisco Blvd. East, San Rafael, CA 94901-5506, USA

Actors in Cover Photograph: Left-to-Right: Back Row: Eric Stiles, Kelsey Marie, Matt T. Baker Middle Row: Emily Rose, Ashley Walton, Calob Lostutter, Saroya Whatley On Shoulders: Kurt Doss Bottom Row: Juliann Lamb, Jonathan Everett, Dianne Benedict
Storyboard Graphic by Patrick Dorsey

Published by: Sandcastle Publishing & Distribution

Post Office Box 3070

South Pasadena, CA 91031-6070

Phone/Website (323) 255-3616, www.sandcastle-online.com

Publisher's Cataloging in Publication

(Provided by Quality Books, Inc.)

Stevens, Chambers.
    The ultimate commercial book for kids & teens : the
young actors' commercial study-guide / Chambers Stevens,
    p. cm. -- (Hollywood 101 ; 6)
    Includes index.
    ISBN: 1-88399-513-2

    1. Television advertising--Vocational guidance.
    2. Television acting--Vocational guidance. I. Title.
    II. Series.

HF6146.T42S843 2005   650.14'024'7914
                   QBI05-800198

First Printing 4/2005

Printed and bound in the United States of America
   09 08 07 06 05   8, 7, 6, 5, 4, 3, 2, 1

What Others Are Saying About The Ultimate Commercial Book

"Chambers Rocks!" Since working with Chambers, I am so much more confident at an audition, because I am well-prepared. I have worked with many other acting coaches, but none of them relate to kids the way he does."**—Stephen Markarina, Actor, Drake and Josh, Ned Declassified**

"Chambers Steven? Enthusiastic, creative, energetic, trustworthy, and knowledgeable about the acting industry. What more could a parent want? Chambers is a masterful teacher that makes learning fun for all his students."

—Bob Wuornos, Gymnastic Coach

"When you've been in the biz as long as I have you've seen actors come and go. But the kids Chambers coach are here to stay."

—Barry Krost, Producer of 16 films including *What's Love Got to Do With It and Love! Valour! Compassion!*

It is so great working with Chambers because he understands how a kid thinks!
—Erica Hartse, 14-year-old Actress, Minneapolis, MN *Tivo, Shop NBC, Knott's Theme Parks*

Chambers is so fun to work with. Funny, too. He helped me book two commercials in two weeks! He's the BEST!
—McKenzie Tingey, 8-year-old Actress, *Las Vegas, NV*

"Chambers has a way of teaching without you feeling that you are being taught. You walk away from him with knowledge that makes you succeed in acting." **—Ross Myrick, 17-year-old Actor, Bakersfield, CA** *Coke, Nintendo, Chevy, Home Depot*

"Chambers Stevens is the best coach I've ever had. He has helped me to not be nervous and to be more outgoing. He has showed me how to let my 'light shine.' He is an inspiration to me and he's funny, too!"

—Amberlynn Dorsey, Actress, *The Cat in the Hat, Hasbro Toys*

The Ultimate Commercial Book for Kids & Teens

What Others Are Saying About Chambers Stevens

"Chambers helped me develop my acting skills in many ways, including broadening my ability to express emotions. He also taught me how to establish a connection with casting directors in the first few seconds of an audition."

—Haley Hessam, 15-year-old Actress, Atlanta, GA
SBC, VOGUE MAGAZINE

"Pure delight! A cut above the rest. Chambers Stevens exudes energy and talent and is a positive force when training young artists. Chambers Stevens . . . a rare industry commodity, indeed."

—Pamela Haynes, Director, West Virginia Film Office

"Chambers is an amazing coach with a funny personality. I knew acting was fun, but with Chambers I didn't know it could be that much fun. He really gets a shy person out of their shell."

—Dana Benedict, Actress, ANNIE IN ANNIE (THE NATIONAL TOUR)

"Chambers is the kind of teacher I wish I had when I was starting out. His passion, energy, and talent guarantees that his students reach their highest potential, and have a great time doing so."

—Larry Zerner, FRIDAY THE 13TH 3-D, FAME

"Chambers' best book to date. A true education course in commercial acting. This book put me on the honor roll. Hollywood 101 is a true winner."

—Jonathan Everett, Actor
HOLES, ATT, THE PAINTED FORREST

"I owe my career to Chambers Stevens."
—Kurt Doss, 6-year-old Actor, 5 national commercials

The Ultimate Commercial Book for Kids & Teens

Table of Contents

The Ultimate Commercial Book for V
Kids & Teens

Dedication

MYRNA LIEBERMAN

WE'VE COME A LONG WAY, BABY!

What do Jennifer Aniston, Britney Spears, Drew Barrymore, Beyoncé, James Cameron, Neve Campbell, Cher, Sheryl Crow, Kirsten Dunst, Sarah Michelle Gellar, Jennifer Love Hewitt, Whitney Houston, KISS, Lenny Kravitz, Lisa Kudrow, Eddie Van Halen, Dustin Hoffman, Oscar De La Hoya, Spike Lee, Madonna, Ricky Martin, Mike Myers, Conan O'Brien, Brad Pitt, Dennis Rodman, Arnold Schwarzenegger, Jerry Seinfeld, Bart Simpson, Sharon Stone, Barbara Streisand, Jonathan Taylor Thomas, Vanessa Williams, Vanna White, and Billy Zane have in common?

They've all done commercials!

For the last fifteen years I have been an acting coach. Just like every professional athlete has a coach, many actors do, too. I have coached young actors in shows for Nickelodeon, WB, CBS, NBC, ABC, and FOX, plus countless movies and theatre productions. I have helped kids get agents, managers, television shows, and even the lead in the school play. But mostly the actors I've coached have worked in commercials. Many of them have done twenty or more. As an actor, I have been in over fifty myself.

I'm sure you are not surprised that there are so many commercial jobs. Everywhere you look there are commercials, commercials, commercials! You can't turn on the television, radio or even go to the movies without running into commercials. Who are all those advertisers trying to reach? Kids and teenagers. In this day and age, young people have more money than ever before. Advertisers know this and want young people to buy their products. How do they do this? They make commercials with kids and teenagers in them. This is where you come in.

The book you are holding is what I've learned coaching over 5,000 kids. It's everything you need to know to get started in commercials. I'll go over how to get an agent, how to get pictures, and even how to audition. Have fun with the commercials in the back of the book. Practice them. Like everything in life, practice makes perfect. Who knows, the next time you turn on your television you might just see yourself.

Question: If your goal is to win a gold medal in the Olympics for wrestling or figure skating, what is the first thing you need to do to reach your goal?

A. Get a sports agent

B. Try out for the Olympic team

C. Learn to wrestle or skate

The answer is obviously C. You will never be able to compete unless you first learn the basics of your sport. It takes a lot of *practice* before you can compete in the Olympics.

This also applies to commercial actors. Before you can get a commercial you need to practice commercials. Lucky for you, you're holding a book that tells you everything you need to know to get started. Plus it has over 150 commercials to work on. So let's get busy.

First let's look at a typical commercial script:

Braces-R-US

They used to call me buck teeth. And I have to admit, I looked a little like a beaver. But after I went to Braces-R-Us, my teeth straightened out. See! *(Actor smiles)* And it didn't bankrupt my parents either. Braces-R-Us. Quality that's affordable.

What is the most important word in this commercial?

If you said "Braces-R-Us" you are right!

In fact, if you wanted to you could rewrite the above commercial just like this:

Braces-R-Us
Braces-R-Us. Braces-R-Us. Braces-R-Us. Braces-R-Us.
Braces-R-Us. Braces-R-Us. Braces-R-Us. Braces-R-Us.
Braces-R-Us. Braces-R-Us. Braces-R-Us. Braces-R-Us.
Braces-R-Us. Braces-R-Us. Braces-R-Us. Braces-R-Us.
Braces-R-Us.

You see, advertisers only care about one thing: selling the viewer on the product. In this case it's an orthodontist's service. So when you practice commercials you have to remember that. If you are not helping them sell the product, you are not doing your job.

Rule #1 - Always remember that commercials are about selling the product.

Now let's work on your first commercial. First thing I want you to do is read it out loud a couple of times.

> ### Eggs
> When my great-grandparents were growing up, they ate eggs every morning. So did my grandparents. So did my parents. But when I was a kid, no eggs. Supposedly all of a sudden they were bad for you. Well, guess what? It turns out they're not bad after all. I don't get it. What were they thinking? Eggs are always good.

Finished? Do you have it memorized yet? If not keep reading it until you've memorized the commercial. Make sure you are reading it out loud. I've found this is the best way to memorize. Often young actors who try to memorize by reading silently, mess up when they first perform it out loud. They get thrown off by the sound of their own voice. Hearing the commercial as you are saying it, really helps memorize it faster. So read it out loud.

EXERCISE: MEMORIZE COMMERCIAL

Is it memorized? If not, DO NOT GO ANY FURTHER!

If you think you have it memorized, I want you to do an exercise.

Stand up. Now do fifteen jumping jacks.

EXERCISE: DO FIFTEEN JUMPING JACKS

Are you a little winded? If not, do fifteen more. Okay, now I want you to do fifteen jumping jacks and say your commercial at the same time.

EXERCISE: DO FIFTEEN JUMPING JACKS WHILE SAYING THE EGGS COMMERCIAL

How did you do? If you didn't mess up at all, you have it memorized. If you messed up...well, sorry, but you don't have it memorized.

You see, if you can do two things at the same time, you have it memorized. When you audition for commercials you will get nervous. Everyone does. Having your commercial memorized, and I mean really memorized, will help you not mess up.

Here is another great exercise to see if you have your commercial memorized. Get a deck of cards. Lay one card from each suit (diamond, hearts, spades, and clubs) face up on the table. As you say your commercial, you are going to sort the cards by suits. Do this very quickly. If you can do this without messing up the cards or the commercial, you have it memorized.

EXERCISE: DO COMMERCIAL WHILE SORTING CARDS

Rule #2 - Memorize your commercial. Test yourself to make sure it is really memorized.

Now here's a brand new commercial. First, memorize it. And then test yourself to make sure you've accomplished your goal.

THE GUITAR METHOD

For Christmas, my parents got me a new guitar. But they said they couldn't afford to get me private lessons. Then I looked in my stocking and found a CD-ROM called "The Guitar Method." It contains over sixty lessons with easy to follow instructions. Within weeks I was doing this. (Actor does a great guitar riff on guitar.) Who needs private lessons when I have "The Guitar Method?"

When you know you have it memorized, stand up. Pick a point on the wall. Make sure you are not standing too close to the point. We're going to pretend this point is the camera. So, you'll want to talk to the camera.

Now, run through your commercial again. Remember, when you say the words "The Guitar Method", smile a little. If *you* don't like the product, then no one else will buy it.

EXERCISE: DO COMMERCIAL LOOKING AT WALL

How did you do? Was it hard talking to the wall? A lot of young actors find this difficult at first. But practice makes perfect. Almost all commercial auditions are on camera. So getting comfortable talking to the camera is very, very important. This is so important that I made it Rule # 3.

Rule #3 - Get comfortable talking to the camera.

Obviously if you have a video camera, you might want to practice with it. Just don't get caught up with how you look. We'll deal with that later. Don't practice looking at the mirror. Mirrors will only distract while you're acting.

The best way to get comfortable talking to the camera is to pretend it's one of your best friends.

Who is your best friend? Standup. Look again at the point on the wall. (Or your video camera) Now, pretend that one of your best friends is standing there. Using the words of the script, tell him/her how much you like eggs.

EXERCISE: DO COMMERCIAL PRETENDING TO TALK TO YOUR BEST FRIEND

Wasn't that easier? I'll bet you were a lot more natural.

Okay, find a CD. Any band will do. You got it? We are going to pretend this CD is "The Guitar Method".

Now the only thing more important than how you *say* the product, is how you *treat* the product. Take a box of cereal for example. It takes tens of thousands of dollars to design a cereal box. The design costs more than most diamonds. Do you understand why the cereal makers want you, the actor, to treat their product with respect?

Rule #4 - Treat the product with respect.

So, hold the CD toward the camera. Make sure your hands aren't covering the front. Now, do the commercial again.

EXERCISE: DO COMMERCIAL USING PROP

How did you do? How did you lay the CD down when you had to pretend to play the guitar? I hope you treated it with respect. It will take some practice. As you're working with props, make sure you hold them high enough. I've found most young actors hold props near their waist instead of near their chest. Turn on the television and look how other actors are using props. See how they are treating the product with respect? With practice, you'll be doing that too. So keep practicing. But before you do, let's go over our four rules.

Rule #1 - **Always remember that commercials are about selling the product.**

Rule #2 - **Memorize your commercial. Test yourself to make sure it is really memorized.**

Rule #3 - **Get comfortable talking to the camera.**

Rule #4 - **Treat the product with respect.**

Okay, now it's time to start practicing.

Warm-up Exercises

Before you start working on your commercials, you need to warm-up. Just like athletes and dancers warm-up before they start their games or performances, actors also need to get their bodies ready to work.

EXERCISE - WARMING UP YOUR BODY

1. Stand up. Pretend you are standing under an apple tree and there is an apple just out of reach. Really reach for it. Do you feel the stretch?

2. Now bend over and touch your toes. Bend your knees just a little. Really feel that stretch.

3. Now run in place for about thirty seconds. Really try to get your heart going and your blood pumping.

Okay, now lets warm up your mouth. Over the years I've found the best way to do this is *tongue twisters*.

EXERCISE - WARMING UP YOUR MOUTH

Repeat each tongue twister five times fast. And I mean fast.

1. Good blood, bad blood

2. Toy boat

3. A big, black bug bit a big, black bear.

4. I slit a sheet, a sheet I slit, upon a slitted sheet I sit.

5. Whether the weather is cold or whether the weather is hot. We will be together whatever the weather, whether you like it or not.

6. Lovely Lucy loves Larry.

7. Peter Piper the pepper picker picked a peck of pickled peppers. A peck of pickled peppers Peter Piper the pepper picker picked. If Peter Piper the pepper picker picked a peck of pickled peppers where's the peck of pickled peppers Peter Piper picked?

   And if you think you're really hot, try this one:

8. Theophilus Thistle, the successful thistle sifter, in sifting a sieve full of unsifted thistles, thrust three thousand thistles through the thick of his thumb. See that thou in sifting a sieve full of unsifted thistles thrust not three thousand thistles through the thick of thy thumb. Success to the successful thistle sifter.

   Did you say each tongue twister five times? If you did, I'll bet you are warmed up now. Okay, time to work on commercials.

Ultimate

Commercials

for Kids & Teens

One Liners

Some commercials just have one line of dialogue. Here are some one liners to practice with. The best way to work on them is to pick any product (cookies, soda pop, makeup, etc.) and use the one liner to express how you feel about the product.

1. Wow!
2. Terrific!
3. Delicious!
4. Mom!
5. Oh, no!
6. Ow!
7. Smells great!
8. Tastes great!
9. That's great, Dad!
10. Good job, Mom!
11. I feel sick!
12. Excellent!
13. It's nice and gooey!
14. All right!
15. Mom! My stomach hurts!
16. Dad!
17. Fantastic!
18. Ow! My head hurts.
19. No!
20. Yes!

Commercials for Girls

All right girls, here are your commercials. Practice with props (magazines, lipstick, etc.). You need to be very comfortable using props on camera. And don't forget to smile. Not a big fake smile. That's worse than no smile at all. Let us know you are having a good time.

Note: Depending on your age, some of the following commercials may be too young or old for you. Skip the ones that don't fit your age group.

21. THE MONEY CARD

Dad said, "You're getting older, you need a credit card." I said, "No, I don't need just any credit card. I need The Money Card." Then my Mom said, "That's my girl."

22. THE DIZZY CHANNEL
(Young girl sitting on a couch. In the background, young kids are watching TV.)

Baby-sitting these guys used to be the hardest job on the planet. That is until they got The Dizzy Channel. Now, I just park these little runts right in front of the tube. And they stay there until it's time to go to bed. And because it's Dizzy, you don't have to worry about it rotting their brain cells. *(Turning around to yell at the TV.)* Go kids, go!

23. GOOEY BARS

I hate to say that I like Snickers bars but...I LOVE GOOEY BARS!!!!!!!!!!!! Sorry, I can't help it....I LOVE GOOEY BARS!!!!!!!!!!! My Mom says screaming is not very lady like. She's right....I LOVE GOOEY BARS!!!!!

24. YUMMY LIP GLOSS

My teacher says, "no eating in class." So I wear Yummy Lip Gloss. Thirteen flavors. All Yummy!

25. PET PLANET

My parents won't let me get a cat, a dog, not even a hamster. But they got me Pet Planet tv channel! But I have one question. How do you feed it?

26. BEAD-A-FUN

Tired of shopping for jewelry and seeing only stupid, boring necklaces? Get Bead-A-Fun. Thousands of different beads. Put them together any way you want. Just don't be boring.

27. CINDIES

My older sister wears cowboy boots. My baby sister wears sandals. But I wear Cindies. Pink. 'Cause when it comes down to it, I'm my own girl.

28. FLOWER PUFF BOOKS

I used to hate to read: Harry Potter, Tom Sawyer, Winnie the Pooh. All books about boys. Don't look at me like that. Winnie the Pooh is too a boy. But then my grandma got me the Flower Puff books. Books about girls. Finally.

29. PAINT BY NUMBERS

I can't draw. I can't trace. I know I can't paint. *(Looking at the Paint By Numbers box.)* What's this? Paint By Numbers? Hey, even I can do that.

30. DIAPIES

Having a baby brother around makes your house smell bad. Then Mommy got Diapies. It was just in time. My nose couldn't stand it anymore.

Commercials for Guys

Okay guys, it's your turn. Remember to memorize the commercials word perfect. And practice using hand gestures. In my coaching, I've noticed that most young actors stick their hands in their pockets instead of gesturing. And don't forget to smile. Remember, you are trying to sell the product.

Note: Depending on your age, some of the following commercials may be too young or old for you. Skip the ones that don't fit your age group.

31. THE NUMBER TWO PENCIL

The Number Two Pencil is number one in my book. Perfect for tests, homework, and even drawing a picture of your teacher. *(He holds up a very ugly picture of his teacher.)*

32. MILK

You want strong bones? Drink milk. You want healthy teeth? Drink milk. You want a good tasting drink? Drink Soda. Nah, I'm just kidding. Drink milk.

33. FRANKLIN'S FAT FREE ICE CREAM

I don't like to talk about it, but I used to be fat. I'm talkin' hippo. I couldn't help it, I liked to eat. Then my mom got me Franklin's Fat Free Ice Cream. It tastes just like the real stuff. Now look at me. Not bad huh?

34. TUBE GUIDE

Whenever I'm watching TV, my brother always walks in the room and says, "What else is on?" I used to hate that. Now I just throw him the Tube Guide. Too bad he can't read.

35. BRACES-R-US

They used to call me buck teeth. And I have to admit, I looked a little like a beaver. But after I went to Braces-R-Us, my teeth straightened out. See!

36. 1-555-COLLECT

You want to call that girl you met at soccer camp, but you don't have any money. Use 1-555-COLLECT. If she accepts the charges, she likes you. If she doesn't? Well, there's always that babe from baseball camp.

37. RODEO

My mother doesn't dress me any more. But she still buys my clothes. I mean, I'm a kid and I don't have any money. So I take her to Rodeo. That way, I get what I want. And she still has some money left to buy me a video game.

38. SPORTS LIVE
(Extreme close-up of a Snowboard Junkie)

And this dude was up. We're talking, sky level. And he was like hanging up, like in the blue, and then he comes screaming down on the powder. His board is almost gone, but he pulls it out and off he jams!

Announcer - Extreme sports on SPORTS LIVE - You have to see it to understand what we're talking about.

39. GRANOLA

My dad says if you want to stay healthy, eat a Granola bar. Every time grownups say, "eat it, it's good for you," it tastes horrible. *(He tastes the Granola bar.)* Wow! This can't be right. It tastes too good to be good for you.

40. SIMPLE TOUCH COMPUTERS
(Sitting in front of his computer.)

Video games are for kids. Get a Simple Touch Computer. Play games the way grown ups play. *(Getting real excited.)* Take that and that. Ha, I got you.

41. THE SOUND SHOP

My car's a piece of crap. But my stereo is the best. With an Am/Fm receiver, cassette player, and CD player it can't be beat. Course, I've got the best speakers you can get. How much do you think the whole set up set me back? Only $199. The same price as my car. If you want a good stereo, check out The Sound Shop. Tell them I sent you.

42. SPORTS UNVEILED MAGAZINE

Okay all you wimps, are you a sports fan or not? Do you read Sports Unveiled Magazine 'cause it's got the best coverage of baseball, football, basketball, and hockey? 'Cause it's the only place to find those hard hitting interviews with the newest sports legends? Or do you read it 'cause of the swim suit edition? Ah, you bunch of wimps.

43. VENICE BEACH
(A Surfer Dude with a massive surf board. He is very hyper.)

'Sup dudes? You want to catch some waves? Then head on over to Venice Beach. They've got babes, waves, and the parking is only a buck, man. *(Whispers.)* Hey, dude. Can I borrow a dollar?

44. MERCURY PCS
(A teenage guy is in the front seat of his car. His arm's around his girlfriend.)

My parents are always on my case. *(Mimics his parents in a whiny voice.)* "We never know where you are." So I told 'em to get me a beeper. So they did. But every time they beeped me, I wasn't near a pay phone. So they were like, "You never call us back." So I told them to get me a Mercury PCS phone. It's all digital. And with Mercury's new nationwide network, your call is always clear. So they did. (He leans in to kiss his girlfriend and the phone rings.) Now if they would just stop calling me.

45. AMEBA DISCMAN
(Eric and Jamie are running. Eric is listening to an Ameba Discman.)

Eric: This spring Jamie and I are running our first marathon. We train every day. In all kinds of weather. It can get boring, especially since Jamie isn't much of a talker. So, I got the new Ameba Discman Portable CD Player. With its anti-skip technology, it's perfect for running. And the sound is great. The only problem is Jamie misses our long conversations. Right Jamie? *(Jamie speeds up and runs ahead.)*

46.   SHOWER MATE

(Male wearing football uniform walks into locker room.)

After football practice I smell like a horse.
(Male walking out of shower.)

But after showering with Mountain Forest by Shower Mate, I smell like summer rain. *(Grabbing another guy as he walks into the locker room.)* Ooh. Here, you need this.

47.   DIANTRIN

I walked up to Amy and said, "Hey, how would you like to go out on Saturday night?" She looked me right in the eye and said, "How would you like to get rid of your dandruff?" So I started using Diantrin. It got rid of my dandruff just like that. Now, I'm going out with Heather. What about Amy? Life's too short for rude girls and dandruff.

48.   WILMINGTON ELECTRIC RAZOR

Scrape. Scrape. Scrape. That's what your razor does every time you shave your face. That's why I use a Wilmington Electric Razor. My face is smooth. And I never cut myself. Wilmington, they're number one for a reason.

49.   BENNON ANTIPERSPIRANT

I was at this great party, when I saw this beautiful blonde. So I walked up to her and said, "Hi. I'm Steve." Then she said, "And you smell...bad." It was my antiperspirant. It wasn't working. I started to walk off, when she grabbed me and whispered in my ear, "Call me when you start using Bennon." The next morning I threw away my old antiperspirant and bought Bennon. Oh, and the blonde? She's now my girlfriend.

50. OCEAN MIST FACE CONDITIONER
(He's standing in front of the mirror. He's just finished shaving.)

First you can't wait to shave. After all, it's only once a month. But then it's once a week. And then, every day. That's a lot of wear and tear on your face. Ocean Mist Face Conditioner prepares your face for that daily shave. Feel. Smooth huh?

Public Service Announcements

Public Service Announcements are another form of commercials. Usually they are about serious subjects. When you perform them, try to be as believable as possible. Be careful not to be too serious. Many young actors overplay PSA's. Try saying the lines as simply as possible. Let the words carry the emotion. Give it a try.

51. SMOKING

My grandfather smoked. He died of lung cancer. My father smokes. Guess what? He has lung cancer, too. You think I'm going to start smoking? If you do, you're a bigger idiot than my relatives.

52. DRINKING
(Dusk. Teen, wearing all black, stands in front of a tree.)

It was supposed to be a great party. Everyone was there. And everyone was drinking. A lot. After a while someone said, "Hey, let's all go down to the lake." Some of us made it.

(Pull back to see teen and three others standing in a graveyard.)

Some of us didn't.

(Title card: Don't drink and drive.)

53. LOVE YOURSELF

Look at me. I'm a big girl. You want skinny, you've come to the wrong place. If you're looking for one of those anorexic models that look like the last thing they've eaten is a cracker three days ago, well...that ain't me. I'm big. I'm proud. And hey...I'm the one who's on TV.

(Title card: Be yourself. It's the only self you've got.)

54. STAY SOBER—1

Drugs are simple. You use them. You ruin your life. What could be simpler than that?

55. STAY SOBER—2

Drugs are simple. Abuse them and you'll die. What could be simpler than that?

56. PREGNANCY
(Screen is black. We hear a baby crying loudly. A young girl or guy walks onto the screen. For about thirty seconds he/she tries to endure the sound of the baby crying. Finally he/she speaks.)

I thought I was ready for sex. But I'm not ready for this.

57. AMNESTY INTERNATIONAL

He was seventeen and sentenced to prison for life. He went to a demonstration to protest the government closing his school. He wanted to learn. He wanted to be educated. He wanted to make something of his life. Now he'll spend it in prison.

Announcer: Amnesty International. Get involved. You can make a difference.

58. TEEN LINE

(Extreme closeup of two teens.)

Teen 1	-	You've got a problem? Call me.
Teen 2	-	You're feeling down? Call me.
Teen 1	-	Your parents are on your case again? Call me.
Teen 2	-	You're thinking about suicide? Call me.
Both Teens	-	Call us. 310-555-1235
Teen 1	-	The Teen Line.
Teen 2	-	We can help.

59. PBS

When I was a kid, every morning I'd get up and watch Sesame Street. I learned the alphabet from the letter of the day. *(Doing the Sesame Street voice)* "Today's show is brought to you by the letter A." Oh, and I learned to count from The Count. *(The Count's voice)* One! Two! Three! Three cupcakes! It was great! When I got to school, I already knew how to read and count. They're not kidding when they say it's educational television.

60. HEART SOCIETY

He ate a lot of red meat. And he didn't get much exercise. In fact, none. That's why he was so overweight. So when Dad had a heart attack, I can't say I was surprised. Thank God he got to the hospital fast. The doctors...they saved his life. Now you should see him. Exercises every day. Follows the Heart Society's recommendations for a healthy diet. And most importantly, he's living life like he's never lived it before.

61. KEEP EARTH BEAUTIFUL

Don't do it because some rock star told you to. Don't do it because some sports hero on TV said he (she) did it. Do it because you know it's right. Because Earth is the only planet we've got.

62. HANDGUNS

(This commercial is a voice over only. The television screen is black.)

Really, my little brother is a great guy. But sometimes he just flies off. Screams and stuff. It's his temper. He doesn't think. So this was one of those times. And he's yelling and yelling and then he runs out of the room. And in a minute he's back with Dad's hand-gun. Dad keeps it around for...I don't know why...I guess to protect us. And Dad thought he had hid it well. But my brother points it at us and starts shooting. (GUN SHOTS.) I guess we were the ones that needed protecting.

63. SAY NO

(A guy and girl are talking in an alley. He has her pressed against a wall.)

Guy - So you wanna do it?
Girl - No.
Guy - You need to loosen up. You wanna smoke?
Girl - No.
Guy - How about a drink?
Girl - No.
Guy - Is that all you ever say, "No?"
Girl - No.

(Guy walks off. Teen girl looks right at the camera.)

Girl - Say no! It isn't that hard.

64. VOTE

I don't get it. Adults who don't vote. Don't they care about this country?

Announcer: Vote on November 2nd. If you care.

65. BOAT SAFETY

When you're on a boat, wear a life jacket. Simple, huh? Well, 55 people this year just didn't get it. No life jacket. No life.

(Camera pans to a sign that says, "55 people died in this lake this year. They all were not wearing life jackets.")

66. SPAYED AND NEUTERED

My grandpa took me to the pound to get a dog. There were hundreds to choose from. But he said I could only have one. He said the rest would be "put to sleep." In other words, killed. I asked why. Because, he said, "people don't spay and neuter their dogs." I don't know what that means. But you better do it.

67. ELECTRIC SAFETY

Before my mother brought home my little brother, we had to baby-proof the house. She said if we didn't, the baby could get hurt.

(A black screen appears with the words.)

Accidents happen.

(It then changes to—)

Don't let them happen to you.

68. JERRY'S KIDS

Every Labor Day weekend, Jerry Lewis has a telethon for kids who have Multiple Sclerosis. Give money. The kids need it.

69. STAY IN SCHOOL

(You see an extreme close up of a teenager.)

Go ahead, quit school. It's stupid. The teachers don't know anything. Get on with your life. I did.

(The camera pulls back and we see the teenager is in jail.)

70. TOUCH

Your body is your own. If someone touches you and makes you feel uncomfortable, tell them to stop. If they don't, tell your parents. Or your teachers. It's your body.

71. WRITE YOUR SCHOOL BOARD

Schools across the country are trying to cut programs. Gym. Music. Theatre. Don't let them. Write your school board. Let your voice be heard.

Most commercials have more than one person in them. So grab a partner and work on these. Once you've perfected the commercial, switch roles. Also, try using props. You want to be prepared for anything that may happen at an audition.

72. COVER UP BY PEARL

(Steve and Kirk in the aisle of a drugstore.)

Steve - Kirk, what's wrong with your face?

Kirk - I've been eating greasy food all week and my skin just can't hack it.

Steve - If Debbie sees that zit, she's going to dump you for sure.

Kirk - I know. What do I do?

Steve - *(Stopping in front of the Cover Up aisle.)* How about trying Cover Up by Pearl. Just pick one that matches your skin tone...

Kirk - *(Selecting a bottle.)* This one looks right.

Steve - ...then put in on your zit. And...

Kirk - It's gone.

Steve - No Kirk. It's Covered Up. By Pearl.

73. HELP.COM

(Brenda and Frieda are at school.)

Frieda - *(Looking at her report card.)* Oh no, a D minus again. But I studied. What did you get?

Brenda - An A.

Frieda - I don't get it. I'm smarter than you. And I know I study more. How do you make such good grades?

Brenda - Help.com. It's a web service staffed by certified teachers. So whenever I need help, I just log on to Help.com.

Frieda - You are so smart.

74. OIL-A-CHANGE #1

Chip - Dad, can I borrow the car?

Charlie - *(Handing him the keys.)* Sure, but first you have to change the oil.

Chip - How do you do that?

Charlie - Well, you need to get a special wrench. We don't have one, so you need to pick one up at the store. Oh yeah, get a new oil filter, too. Then we need to find some way to jack the car up a couple of feet. Then...

Chip - Wait, that's a lot of work. Isn't there an easier way?

Charlie - You could take it to Oil-A-Change. They'll do the whole job in fifteen minutes. And it's only $19.95.

Chip - Great idea. Can I borrow twenty dollars?

75. OIL-A-CHANGE #2

(Gwen enters. Her dad, Charlie, is reading the newspaper.)

Gwen - *(Handing him the keys.)* Here Dad. Thanks for letting me borrow the car.

Charlie - Young lady, you are fifteen minutes past curfew. You better have a good excuse or you're grounded.

Gwen - I went to Oil-A-Change. They changed the oil, rotated my tires, and even installed new windshield wiper blades. All in just fifteen minutes. So what do you have to say about that, Dad?

Charlie - Why can't your brother be more like you?

76.   CHEF BOY'S PIZZA

(Two teenagers enter the house.)

Teen 1 -   What's that great smell?
Teen 2 -   My mom probably made homemade pizza again.
Teen 1 -   Homemade? You've got to be kidding.
Teen 2 -   No. She's just a big pal of the Chef Boy.
            You want a piece?
Teen 1 -   *(Taking a piece and then tasting it.)* Do you think she could
            introduce my mom to the Chef?

(They laugh.)

77. CML BEEPERS

(Two teenagers are walking down a school hallway.)

Girl -   Wow! When did you get a beeper.
Guy -   Last week.
Girl -   I can't believe your parents bought you one.
Guy -   No, I bought it myself. They have this great deal at CML
          beepers. Only eight dollars a month and they give you
          the beeper.
Girl -   Yeah, but don't they charge you every time you get
          paged?
Guy -   Nope. Unlimited paging. And for a couple of dollars
          more, you can get one that accepts text messages.
Girl -   When did you get so smart?

(They laugh and continue down the hall.)

78. HOMEMADE SOUP

(Heather's in the kitchen doing her homework, when Suzanne walks in.)

Suzanne - *(Entering.)* It smells great.

Heather - It's Homemade Chicken Noodle Soup.

Suzanne - You're lucky to have a Mom that is such a great cook.

Heather - No, I made it.

Suzanne - No!

Heather - Yes! All you do is open a can.

Suzanne - *(Tasting the soup.)* But it tastes homemade.

Heather - That's because it is.

79. GOOEY BARS

(Two teenagers who look totally different.)

Twin 1 - Being a twin is...

Twin 2 - ...hard. Everyone's always...

Twin 1 - ...staring at us and saying...

Twin 2 - ..."Are you guys twins?"

Twin 1 - Like, duh!

Twin 2 - Like, really duh!

Twin 1 - But really, we're a lot more different than we...

Twin 2 - ...look. Especially when it comes to...

Twin 1 - ...candy bars. I like...

Twin 2 - Gooey Bars.

Twin 1 - No, I'm the one who likes Gooey Bars!

Twin 2 - You do? Well I guess we are a lot alike.

Two-Person Commercials

80. PURRFECT CLOTHES
(Crystal and Evoe meet in the hall.)

Crystal - What happened to you?

Evoe - What?

Crystal - Yesterday you were like this nerd and now you're...almost cute.

Evoe - It's the clothes. They're Purrfect.

Crystal - You're telling me. Hey, do you want to go out?

81. ARCANE PENS
(Frannie and Jesse are in class taking a test.)

Jesse - Can I borrow a pen?

Frannie - Do you want an Arcane Rolling Ball or an Arcane Precise?

Jesse - Whatever.

Frannie - The Arcane Rolling Ball comes in five different colors. Red, black, green, purple, and blue.

Jesse - ...Okay...

Frannie - But the Arcane Precise has a finer line for those hard to take tests.

Jesse - Look I just need to borrow a pen. Even a pencil will do.

Frannie - Do you want an Arcane Number 1 or an Arcane Number 2?

Announcer - People get excited about our pens and pencils.

82. CANCER WALK

Kid one - Wanna help raise money for cancer research?
Kid two - Walk in the Cancer Walk this Saturday at
Highland Park!
Kid one - You can make a difference!
Kid two - Sign up today.

83. SLIM CUISINE

Girl - To gain weight or not to gain weight?
That is the question.

Boy - Then what's the answer?

Girl – Slim Cuisine.

84. BROCCOLI

(Evan and Jamie are eating lunch in the cafeteria. Evan is eating cafeteria food. And Jamie brought his lunch.)

Evan - What did you bring for lunch?
Jamie - Broccoli!
Evan - You're kidding.
Jamie - Why would I kid about my favorite vegetable?
Evan - You're strange.
Jamie - Hey, you're the one eating cafeteria food.
Look at your plate.
Evan - *(Looking at his lunch.)* Do you think I could have
some broccoli?

KES

, a bowl of cereal when Justin enters.)

Justin - You better not have eaten all the Sweet Flakes!
Ashley - *(Her mouth is full.)* I didn't!!!!
Justin - *(Holding up the empty box.)* Then how do you explain this?
Ashley - *(Chewing fast.)* I was hungry?
Justin - Ahhhh!

(Justin chases Ashley out of the room.)

Announcer - Sweet Flakes. If you want a happy house, you better buy two boxes.

86. WART AWAY
(Tiara is looking at her hand when Sarah enters.)

Sarah - Are you picking at your wart again?
Tiara - No. Look, it's gone.
Sarah - How did that happen?
Tiara - Wart Away.
Sarah - That's amazing.
Tiara - No, it's Wart Away.

87. RECYCLE

Kid one - You want to help the earth?
Kid two - Recycle.
Kid one - You want help your neighborhood?
Kid two - Recycle.
Kid one - Yeah, Recycle.
Kid two - It will help.

88. PRIMO MICROWAVES
(Bret and Mikie are playing videogames. They both reach for the popcorn bowl. It's empty.)

    Bret - We need more popcorn.
    Mikie - Yep.
    Bret - Then make some.
    Mikie - How?
    Bret - Just put the popcorn in the microwave and push popcorn.
(At that moment Mikie's videogame character dies.)
    Mikie - I wish this game were that easy.

Announcer - Primo Microwaves. We make cooking easy.

89. BURRITO BELL
(Laurel and Marsha are standing at the Burrito Bell counter.)

    Laurel - I think I want a taco.
    Marsha - Make that two.
    Laurel - And maybe a burrito.
    Marsha - Make that two.
    Laurel - And a steak enchilada
    Marsha - Really?
    Laurel - They're really good.
    Marsha - Then make that two.

Announcer - Friends helping friends. At Burrito Bell.

90. DIRT BE GONE

(Girl runs in to find boy doing laundry.)

Girl - I heard it, but I didn't believe it.
Boy - My mom says I dirty up too many clothes.
Girl - So she's making you do the laundry?
Boy - It bites. I'll never get these stains out.
Girl - Sure you will. Just use Dirt Be Gone. One cup and no more stains.
Boy - How did you get so smart?
Girl - My mom makes me do the laundry, too.

(They laugh.)

91. CHOCOLATE ICE

Guy - Knock, knock.
Girl - Who's there?
Guy - Chocolate Ice.
(The girl doesn't say anything.)
Guy - Aren't you going to say, "Chocolate Ice, who?"
Girl - No dummy. Everybody knows what Chocolate Ice is.

Announcer – When you're the best Chocolate Ice Cream in the world, no one can forget you.

Some commercials are crazy. MTV and Nickelodeon are full of silly commercials. Here are some for you to practice with. Have fun with them.

92. TUXEDO CENTER

It's not every day that you get to go to the prom with the best looking babe in school. I mean, look at me, why would she want to go out with me? Could it be I told her I was going to pick her up in a limo? Nope. Could it be the dozen roses I sent her? Sorry, that's not it. Actually, I let it slip I was getting my tux from the Tuxedo Center. She went wild. "Yes! Yes! Please take me. I'm yours!" She couldn't help it. I do that to some people.

93. GIRLS SPORTS OF AMERICA

Okay girls, go out there and PLAY SOME BALL. Let's kick some butt. Let's beat some bootie. Let's smash some faces. But remember, be nice.

Announcer - Girls Sports of America. We teach you how to kick butt...nicely.

94. COOL GUM

I used to be a nerd, geek, dork, jerk. All the kids at school called me...dimwit, dumbbell, nincompoop, stooge. That was until I discovered Cool Gum. One chew and I went from fool to cool. So before you get beat up for wearing high waters, get your cool gum today.

Crazy Commercials

95. CAT-A-BUTTER

My cats are always bugging me. Meow! Meow! Meow! Meow! Meow! From the way they tell it, you would think they were always starving. Then I got new Cat-A-Butter from Whisko. It's a peanut butter for cats. One spoonful and their little mouths gets so gummed up that they can't meow all day. And they like the tuna peanut butter taste. So, if you need some peace and quiet, try new Cat-A-Butter.

96. SPIDO BATHING SUITS
(For guys.)

Have you ever had a girl follow you around? Like she likes you or something? It's disgusting isn't it? They're always looking at you, smiling and laughing at your jokes. What do they want, a boyfriend? I used to have that problem 'til I got a bathing suit from Spido. Smaller than a Speedo. A Spido is guaranteed to gross out that pesky girl. They come in five different colors but only one size. Extra, extra small. Spido. Guaranteed to gross the girl out.

97. CLIP NOTES

Homework bites! It's bad enough we have to go to school seven hours a day. But then, they give you three hours of homework! Teachers are so cruel. Luckily, I have Clip Notes. Clip Notes are for those days when you don't feel like doing your homework. Look, say your teacher wants you to read TO KILL A MOCKING-BIRD and then write a report on it. All you have to do is pick up the Clip Notes for the book and you're all set. Each Clip Notes includes a summary of the book. Plus there are a couple of book reports you can turn in as your own in the back. Just so your teacher doesn't suspect anything, a couple of words are purposely misspelled. Clip Notes. You'll never have to do homework again.

98. BEANS

They call beans the musical fruit. Oh come on, you've heard that. But so what? What's wrong with eating food that plays a little music. I would think that would be a real good selling point. Imagine a hamburger that after you eat it plays "Stairway to Heaven." Or French fries that harmonize. It will never happen. 'Cause only beans are the musical fruit. Oh! Gotta go! I feel a song coming on.

99. DIAL-A-PARENT

Spokesperson - Are your parents ever mean to you? Like they never let you go out on weekends? And during the week, they make you do your homework? And the nagging. "Clean your room. Feed the cat. Get in here and help me change grandpa's diaper!" It's enough to drive you crazy. Don't you wish you could go back to the days when your parents were nice to you? Well, you can with Dial-A-Parent. Watch.

(Spokesperson dials the phone. We hear the voice on the other end.)
Parent - Get off the phone and get your butt in here and help me
        clean the litter box.
Spokesperson - *(Hanging up.)* Uh-oh, wrong number.

100. THE ROMANCE NETWORK
(Guy crying in front of the television.)

And then this lady loses her daughter 'cause she used to be messed up with this disease that makes her like crazy. And then she meets this doctor and they like make out and she's better and she wants her daughter baaaaaaaaaaaaaaaaaaaaaack.

Announcer - The Romance Network is for women. 'Cause guys just don't understand.

Crazy Commercials

(Valley Girl holding a can of Diet Pop.)

Have you like seen those lame soft drink ads where like some chick like tries to tell you that the diet drink she's like holding like tastes as good as like the non diet drink she like usually likes?

(She sips the Diet Pop.)

Well, they're like very good commercials.

102. Whopper King

My girlfriend says I can never make up my mind about anything. That's totally not true. At least, I don't think it is. Though my other girlfriend did say the same thing last night. But there is one thing I know I like. A Jumbo from Whopper King. Unlike some fast food restaurants, Whopper King makes every Jumbo fresh. Just the way I like them. With cheese. Sometimes with cheese. Sometimes without. Sometimes I like tomatoes on them, too. Sometimes I don't. Sometimes....

103. Angel Tissues

(She lets out a big sneeze.)

Cold season is not fun. *(She sneezes again.)* Especially if you get a chapped nose. Angel tissues have lotion weaved into every tissue. *(She sneezes again.)* Every time I sneeze, my nose gets a little soothing comfort. Angel makes cold season not so bad. *(She sneezes again.)*

104. BLADES

You ever had one of those haircuts that's too long on one side and too short on the other? Or the person messes it up so bad that you have to wear a hat for a month? I've been all over town looking for someone who knows how to cut hair. It was getting so bad the people at school gave me this. *(Camera pans down. He is wearing a shirt that says: Permanent Bad Hair Day.)* Then I found Blades for men. You never need an appointment. And every haircut is guaranteed or your money back. Now I just need someone who'll shave my back.

105. ANTI-ZIT CREAM

My best friend Tasha is so cute. But her skin. Well...she needed help. I told her about Anti-Zit Cream. It not only covers up your blemishes, but dries them out. Well, Tasha tried it. And now her skin looks great. So great that she stole my boyfriend.

106. FLIRT CARDS
(A geeky guy is standing in front of his locker.)

Guy Geek - Do you have trouble meeting babes? Every time you get around them, you talk like a blooming idiot? I used to have that problem until I got Flirt Cards by Renco. Flirt Cards are easy to use and girls love them. All you do is walk up to a girl. And read from the cards. *(He walks up to a geeky girl standing by her locker.)*

Guy Geek - *(Looking at the cards.)* Did it hurt?
Girl Geek - Did what hurt?
Guy Geek - When you fell from heaven.
Girl Geek - That is so cute. Would you like to go out with me on Saturday night?
Guy Geek - Sure. *(The girl walks away.)*
Guy Geek - See, works every time.

Crazy Commercials

107. BREATH MINTS
(Michael is holding Katie in his arms.)

Michael - Katie you are so beautiful.
Katie - *(Flirting.)* Stop it.
Michael - You are. How would you like to hook up later?
Katie - How about now?
Michael - Okay, but do you have a breath mint?
Katie - Your breath isn't bad.
Michael - No, but yours is. Stinky.

108. MUSCLE-ADE
(Teen one and Teen two run into the kitchen. They've been on a long distance run.)

Teen one - I won!
Teen two - How did you get so fast? Last week I kicked your butt.
Teen one - *(Opening the fridge.)* Muscle-Ade!
Teen two - I've never heard of it.
Teen one - *(Handing Teen two a Drink)* Taste it.
Teen two - *(Spitting it out.)* That's terrible.
Teen one - Yeah, but it's good for you! *(Flexing muscle.)* Look at this.
Teen two - What's in this drink?
Teen one - Muscles.
Teen two - *(Starting to get worried)* Muscles? What kind of muscles?
Teen one - Cows. Horses. Some really strong pigs. You want another drink?

(Teen two throws up, then faints.)

42 The Young Actors' Commercial Study-guide!

Copyright © 2005 by Chambers Stevens

109. CLEAN PIPES IN A JAR!
(Erin is standing in the front yard when Avery walks up.)

Avery - What's the plumber doing at your house again?
That's three times this week.

Erin - My dad keeps clogging up the pipes.
I told him not to eat that ten pound prime rib.

Avery - You know what you need? Clean Pipes In A Jar! Just
empty the jar and after a small explosion, your pipes
will be clean.

Erin - Thanks. But what do we do about the smell?

Avery - Keep your dad away from the prime rib.

110. CINNAMON TOOTH FLOSS

Girl - Ooh, what is that in your teeth?

Boy - I was eating a hamburger and I have sesame seeds
between my teeth.

Girl - Then why don't you floss or something?

Boy - Because I just ran out of Cinnamon Floss. And I'd
rather let my teeth rot than use anything else.

Girl - From the way your breath smells, I think your teeth
have already rotted.

111. GASO
(Justin and Crystal are in an elevator full of people.)

Justin - Excuse me, did you just let one?

Crystal - Could you speak a little softer? It's not my fault
I have gas.

Justin - Yes it is. You should take Gaso.

Crystal - What's that?

Justin - Gaso is a food enzyme that helps stop gas before it starts.

Crystal - So the next time I eat Mexican food...

Justin - Eat Gaso first.

Practice Commercials

Do you need more practice? Here are forty more commercials. These work for guys or girls. Keep practicing. That's the only way to get better.

112. BOLKSVAGEN BUG

So I told my mom, look, instead of giving me your old car, why don't you get me a new Volkswagen Bug? She said, "I've got a better idea. Why don't I give you the old junker and I'll get a new Bolksvagen Bug." Don't you just hate smart parents?

113. FANTASTICMUSIC.NET

Log on to fantasticmusic.net. You'll find more than 4,000 artist mini sites with bios, lyrics, sound clips, and exclusive photographs. But here's the best part. They've got full length music videos on demand. Fastasticmusic.net, it's everything you'd expect from your favorite magazine.

114. 11-11-321

11-11-321. Now for only eight cents a minute! Just dial 11-11-321 before your long distance number and bam, you'll get that great eight cents a minute savings. Did I mention it was only eight cents a minute? See if this commercial was a phone call, it would only cost you eight cents. So dial 11-11-321 today.

115. EGGS

When my great-grandparents were growing up, they ate eggs every morning. So did my grandparents. So did my parents. But when I was a kid, no eggs. Supposedly all of a sudden they were bad for you. Well, guess what? It turns out they're not bad after all. I don't get it. What were they thinking? Eggs are always good.

44 The Young Actors' Commercial Study-guide!

116. BROOKS MACARONI AND CHEESE

I hate to cook, but I love to eat. Which is a huge problem when you've got a Mom like mine. "This is not a restaurant. If you want to eat, then learn to cook." So I did. It was either that or starve. But guess what? It wasn't as hard as I thought. With Brooks Macaroni and Cheese, all you do is boil water, pour in the contents of the box, and you have great macaroni and cheese. I wish laundry was this simple.

117. NEW NAVY

You know what I hate? Trendy people. They've always got to have the latest clothes. Don't they know that everything they buy today will be out of style tomorrow? That's why I only shop at New Navy. They have the classics. That way I'm never out of style.

118. THE BLUES PAGES

When you don't know what from what or who from who. When you don't know the right way to get wherever it is you are going. When you wish you could find that thing you're looking for. Then you only have one choice. The Blue Pages. More than a phone book.

119. LIPSTEX

During the winter, my lips used to always be chapped. It wasn't a pretty sight. That's why I use Lipstex. Lipstex is not just chapstick. It's a medicated lip ointment that heals and protects. To winterize your lips, use Lipstex.

Practice Commercials

120. MARATHON NETWORK

My mom's always saying, "When I was a kid, this" or "When I was a kid, that." And I'm always like, "Yeah, yeah, yeah." Then one day, I'm watching TV and she comes and changes the channel to the Marathon Network. I sat there for five hours watching: Taxi, I Love Lucy, The Jeffersons, The Brady Bunch, All in the Family, Mary Tyler Moore, The Bob Newhart Show, The Partridge Family, The Andy Griffith Show, and Happy Days. Now when she says, "When I was a kid..." I listen.

121. AUDIO/VIDEO SHOP

Stereos, Computers, DVD Players, Big Screen TV's, CD Players, Walkman, Batteries, Video Tapes, VCR's. How many reasons do you need to go to Audio/Video Shop?

122. ALMOND BAR/PECAN BAR
(Teen walks up to a clerk in a convenience store.)

Choices! Choices! Choices! There are too many choices. Do I take band or drama? Do I live with my mom or my dad? Do I work at the Burger Shack or the mall? Do I want an Almond Bar or a Pecan bar?

(The clerk puts an Almond Bar and a Pecan Bar on the counter.)

When it comes to candy I don't worry about choices.

(To Clerk.) I'll take them both.

123. KAPLAN'S CAMERA SHOP
(Teenager runs into his/her parent's bedroom, flips on the lights.)

Dad, Mom, wake up! I've finally decided what I want for graduation. Kaplan's new Mini Digital Video Camera. Mom! Wake up! It's got high resolution computer ready digital video and...Dad you're snoring! Oh, and a 12x optical 48x digital zoom with image stabilization. Guys get up! You can sleep later. Oh, and the best part is it's got a color LCD screen and view finder. *(The parents don't move.)* Okay, forget it. But don't blame me if you miss the half price sale at Kaplan's Camera Shop. *(The parents jump out of bed and run for the door.)* Hey guys! Wait up.

124. THE GUITAR METHOD

For Christmas, my parents got me a new guitar. But they said they couldn't afford to get me private lessons. Then, I looked in my stocking and found a CD-ROM called "The Guitar Method." It contains over sixty lessons with easy to follow instructions. Within weeks I was doing this. *(Actor does a great guitar riff on guitar.)* Who needs private lessons when I have "The Guitar Method?"

125. WRAT

Pink Floyd, The Rolling Stones, Aerosmith, The Beatles, Tom Petty, Bruce Springsteen, Van Halen, Bob Dylan, Jimi Hendrix, Santana. When you want the classics, you want WRAT.

126. FLORIDA'S BEST

I'm no longer a baby. So why should I drink baby drinks? Florida's Best. 100% orange juice. It doesn't get any better than this.

127. THE T-SHIRT SHOPPE

No matter what clothes go in or out of style, you can never go wrong with a T-shirt. At The T-Shirt Shoppe they have over 500 different T-shirts. If you like sports, rock stars, movies, or animation, you can bet that The T-Shirt Shoppe has a T-shirt to fit your needs.

128. TEEN FASHION MAG

(Male or female walks up to the front door of a house. The door opens and out comes an elderly woman with curlers in her hair.)

Hi. I'm from Hendersonville High School and we're selling magazines to help the band. And I was wondering, have you ever thought of subscribing to Teen Fashion? It's like regular fashion magazines, but it has articles, fashion tips, and sizzling pics just for teens. I have an issue, would you like to take a look?

(Cut to teen walking away. The old woman is still on the porch, but this time she is dressed real hip and her hair is blue with pink highlights.)

129. HAWAIIAN PINEAPPLES

You want a taste of sunshine? You want a taste of the tropics? You want to get your daily allowance of Vitamin C? Hawaiian Pineapples. It's the answer.

130. CHICKEN FINGERS

(Looking at a box of Carlson's Chicken Fingers.)

Chickens do not have fingers. Will someone please tell the people at Carlson's that if they are going to put something on the box, they could at least get it right. I mean, you've seen chickens. When was the last time you saw one with hands, much less fingers. *(A plate appears with cooked chicken fingers on it. The Spokesperson takes one.)* Umm...forget what I just said.

131. BDX

At school, they call me the mixmaster. No one can make a mix tape like me. It's not easy finding the perfect balance. Of course, it helps that I use only BDX tapes. So when you want to groove to the beat or slam to the jam, use BDX.

132. AMERICAN INSURANCE

If you've got one of me at home, you might be worrying about how you're ever going to afford car insurance. Car insurance for teenagers can be very expensive. That is, until you call American Insurance. Hey, they covered me.

133. SUBARAMA

My friends and I can never agree on anything. So the only place we go together is Subarama. They have a variety of sandwiches, made hundreds of different ways. Betty likes meatballs. Dolores likes plain-ole ham-and-cheese. Me, I like the Italian sub on wheat. At Subarama you don't have to agree. Because they've got it all.

134. THE UNDERGROUND FASHION MART

Fashion. It can be a trend or a fad. A craze or a rage. But whatever's in vogue, you can bet they have it at The Underground.

135. BUCK'S BURGER SHOPPE
(Extreme close-up of teen, wearing sunglasses, sneaks up to the camera and whispers.)

What would you say if I told you I could get you a hamburger with melted American cheese, tomato, onion, crisp bacon, classic sauce, a charbroiled beef patty between two slices of crunchy sourdough toast? I know what you would say....yum!

(We pull back to see the teen is standing in the parking lot of Buck's Burger Shoppe.)

136. ECHINACEA

My life is busy. The last thing I need is to be knocked down by a cold. So, whenever I feel one coming on, I take Echinacea. It promotes well-being in cold and flu seasons. I never get sick. Just busier.

137. 7 FLAGS
(Every sentence is on a different ride at 7 Flags.)

The best thing about 7 Flags on Tuesdays is that if you bring a diet soda can—. Well, it doesn't have to be diet, it can be regular. As long as it's a can. Oh, they take glass bottles, too. I think they even take plastic bottles. But I'm not positive on that. You'd better call ahead just to make sure. Anyway, the best thing about 7 Flags on Tuesdays is...I forgot.

Announcer: Tuesdays at 7 Flags bring any can or bottle and get ten dollars off the admission price.

138. Juicy Burger

Bacon. Cheese. Bacon. Cheese. It's that simple. A good hamburger has two things. Bacon and cheese...oh, and ketchup. I forgot ketchup. Oh, and lettuce. Oh, and...

Voice Over: Juicy Burger. We make them the way you like them.

139. Little Nero's Pizza
(A bunch of guys hanging around. Our hero jumps up.)

Hero: So guys, what's it going to be? We can call the usual place and get the pizza in thirty minutes or less. Or we can call Little Nero's and get two of the best pizzas in the city for the same price. I don't care. We can call the usual place or we can call Little Nero's. Oh, did I mention Little Nero's has great garlic sticks? But hey, it doesn't matter to me. Just pick one of them, I'm starving. Oh yeah, and Little Nero's has those great...

Announcer: Little Nero's. Pizza for people who love pizza.

140. Spaghetti Yums

When I was kid, I was picky about what I ate. That's why my dad gave me Spaghetti Yums. The perfect food for the picky eater.

141. Instant Oatmeal

My mom has to be at work before I even get out of bed. But she still worries about what I eat. Instant Oatmeal, it's good. And it stops your mom from worrying.

Practice Commercials

142. THE PARTY PLACE

Your birthday. Christmas. Halloween. New Years. St. Patrick's Day. Thanksgiving. Lincoln's Birthday. Valentine's Day. Fourth of July. The Party Place has got you covered.

143. BETWEEN THE LINES

Imagine a store where you can paint your own plates. Cups. Mugs. Bowls. Between The Lines. A different kind of store.

144. SNACKIES

(Holding a Snackie.) When I heard they were making Snackies with chocolate in the middle, I said, "It will never work." *(Tasting the Snackie.)* Okay, it works. Who thought of this? *(Taking another bite.)* You got any more? Hey you, behind the camera. I need another Snackie.

145. SLURPINS

When I was a kid, I drank soda. Lots and lots of soda. The caffeine made me bounce off the walls. Now I drink Slurpins. 'Cause what you drink, should taste good. It shouldn't make you crazy.

146. FUN FLAKES (MADE WITH REAL CORN)

My aunt eats Fun Flakes. My uncle eats Fun Flakes. All my cousins eat Fun Flakes. *(The camera pulls back to show the actor eating Fun Flakes.)* I guess it runs in the family.

147. NIBBLE BITS

Ziggy, my cat, only eats the best. So my parents buy Nibble Bits. *(Holding up Ziggy.)* Hear that? She's purring. She wants her Nibble Bits.

148. APPLES

I don't know if an apple a day keeps the doctor away. But I do know that an apple a day is a great snack. Especially if it has peanut butter on it. Hey, do you think peanut butter keeps the doctor away, too?

149. YOGURT

Did you know that the oldest person in the world died when she was one hundred and thirty? Guess what she ate every day? Yogurt. So if you want to live a long time, eat up.

150. WHIPPIN CREAM

Whippin Cream goes great on anything. Steak. Potatoes. Pizza. *(Looking off camera.)* What? Oh, only desserts. Sorry. Whippin Cream goes great on anything. Cake. Brownies. Cookies. *(Looking off camera again.)* Is that better? *(Walking off camera.)* You know, I bet Whippin Cream would taste good on Pizza.

151. CANTALOUPE

You're looking at my breakfast. Cantaloupe. I know what you're thinking. But it's good. No, not good. Great. So next time you are at the supermarket, grab one. Your stomach will thank you later.

Getting

an

Agent

Have you been practicing your commercials? Can you perform them smoothly and naturally? Can you memorize quickly? If you answered *yes*, then you are ready for the next big step in your commercial career. If your answers are *no*, don't read further. You will be wasting your time. Agents aren't that hard to get. But they are almost impossible to get if you're not prepared.

So how do you get an agent? Well, it is not as difficult as most people think. First you have to know that agents *need* talented actors. If the agents don't have good actors, they don't make any money. And since the young actors they do have are constantly growing up, the agents are always on the look out for their newest star. Who knows, that could be you.

Now before I tell you how to get an agent, let me tell you what an agent is and what an agent is not.

An agent is —

1. someone who submits you for commercial auditions.
2. someone who negotiates your salary when you book the commercial.

For that, they take ten percent of the money you make from the commercial job. (In some of the smaller cities, they take fifteen percent.)

Getting an Agent

An agent doesn't —

1. get jobs for you. If an agent promises you jobs, then they aren't being honest with you.
2. take money from you *before* you get a job. If the agent asks for money before you get a job—run! He/she is not really an agent.

Okay, now that you know what an agent is and doesn't do, it's time to tell you how to get in touch with one. First, you need to know what agents are in your area. There are a couple of easy ways to do this.

1. First, try the internet. The free websites I would check first are www.sag.org and www.aftra.org. These are the union websites. So you can trust the agencies listed there.

2. Another excellent site is www.hcdonline.com. This is the Hollywood Creative Directory. They sell many wonderful books that are updated regularly. The one you will want to buy is the Hollywood Representation Directory. It lists over 2,000 agents and managers around the country.

3. One other source is your state film commission. Every state has one. You can find your state at The Association of Film Commissioners website:

www.afci.org. The film commission's job is to bring the motion picture industry into their state. Each commission has a film resource directory, listing the services in their state. Give them a call and ask them to send you one. It will contain the agents in your area.

So you now know how to find an agent. Pick one and write him/her a letter.

Simple, huh? Remember what I told you. Agents are always on the lookout for the next great young actor. Now, of course, with the letter, you need to enclose a picture of yourself. (I'll go into that later.) If the agent is looking for your type and age, then they will call you and set up an audition.

Sounds easy, doesn't it?

Here is an example of a letter you can write.

Sample Agent Letter #1

Date
Agent's Name
Agent's Company
Agent's Address

Dear (Agent's Name):

My name is Frankie Black and I'm looking for an agent. I read in the book *Ultimate Commercials for Kids and Teens* that you are one of the best agents in *(insert the name of your town)*. Well guess what? I'm one of the best young actors in *(insert town)*. I recently played the lead in a production of <u>Grease</u> at my school. It was a big hit. Even my dad liked it and he hates musicals. I also have been studying acting for a number of years. How about letting me come in and do a commercial for you?

See you soon,

Frankie Black

This letter works because it's funny, short, and to-the-point.

Now it's time to write your own letter. Notice I did not say, "Now it is time to have your parents write your letter." If you are old enough to read this book, then you are old enough to write your own agent letter. And the many agents I've talked to say they like getting letters from young actors better than getting one from their parents.

EXERCISE - WRITE AN INTRODUCTION LETTER TO AN AGENT

Here are the important things to include.

1.   Your name

2.   A little bit about yourself. Maybe your age. Where you go to school. Any plays you recently have been in.

3.   That you are looking for an agent.

4.   How you heard about them.

5.   And ask them if you can come in and do a commercial for them. (This will tell them you know what it takes to audition.)

Keep your letter short. One paragraph is plenty.

A note here: if you don't get a response within two weeks, then write another agent. Then another. Until you find one that will respond. If they don't respond, send another picture. Or maybe give them a call and find out why they didn't respond.

Now, what happens when you visit an agent?

After an agent has read your letter, seen your picture, calls you, and asks you to come in for a meeting, then what happens? Well, this is where your weeks of practicing commercials comes in. Most agent meetings go something like this:

Agent walks into the waiting room where Michael and his parents have been sitting.

Agent   -   Hello. I'm Lori Beth Bernat. You must be Michael?
Michael -   Yes. Nice to meet you.
Agent   -   Come on back to my office.
             (To Michael's parents) Why don't you just wait here.

The agent takes Michael into her office.

Agent   -   So...you want to be in commercials?

Michael	-	Absolutely. I love to act. I've been the lead in a couple of plays at school. We just did <u>Godspell</u> at my church, and I was Peter.
Agent	-	So you can sing?
Michael	-	Well, I'm not very good. But I can rap. You want to hear me?
Agent	-	Sure.

(Michael raps.)

Agent	-	Great. You know, last week we were casting a Burger King commercial, and we were looking for a guy who could rap. Too bad I didn't know you then.
Michael	-	Would you like to see a commercial I've been working on?
Agent	-	Okay. It's not long is it?
Michael	-	No, it's short.
Agent	-	Let's see it. (Then the phone rings and she answers the phone. After fifteen minutes, she hangs up.) Okay, I'm ready.

(Michael performs a commercial. Since he's been practicing, he's brilliant.)

Agent	-	Fantastic. Let's go talk to your parents.

———

Getting an Agent

I have sent hundreds of kids to interview with agents and most of the time, this is exactly how the interview goes.

Let's go through all the things Michael did right.

1.   *Michael was nice and courteous with the agent.*
     Remember, the agent has to like you to represent you.

2.   *When the agent suggested that Michael leave his parents in the lobby, he did not complain.*
     Most agents want to see the actor alone. They want to see how you handle yourself *without* your parent's help. Parents tend to dominate the interview. Do yourself a favor; leave them in the lobby. (A note to the parents: if it makes you uncomfortable to leave your child alone with a stranger, tell the agent this.)

3.   *Michael was very talkative.*
     Every time the agent asked him a question, he not only answered it but he *kept talking*. When you are talkative, it shows that you have confidence. Of course, it is also important to be a good listener.

4.   *Michael told the truth.*
     He knew he couldn't sing, so he told the truth. Don't lie to your agent. I once had a kid who lied

to his agent. He told her he could skateboard when he couldn't. The agent sent him on a Pepsi audition where he had to skateboard. The kid broke his arm.

5. *Michael turned all negatives into positives.*
    The agent asked *Michael* if he could sing.
    Michael said, "Well, not very good." But then he went on to tell the agent about the things HE COULD DO, like rap. Agents need kids with many skills. *Michael* scored points here by showing the agent that he is multi-talented.

6. *Michael asked to do a commercial.*
    After *Michael* was sure that the agent liked him, he offered to do a commercial. Why? Because the bottom line is: commercials are what the agent will be representing you for. So *Michael*, after having worked for weeks, felt confident in his ability to perform. The agent was impressed.

EXERCISE - GET ONE OF YOUR PARENTS TO INTERVIEW YOU

Follow *Michael's* example by:

° Being nice and courteous.
° Being talkative.
° Answering every question with a full, complete answer.

° Tell them about your many skills.
° Volunteer to do a commercial.

NOTE TO PARENTS: Interview your kid by asking him/her
the following questions:

1.   What grade are you in?
2.   What school do you go to?
5.   Why do you want to be an actor?
6.   What kind of acting have you done before?
7.   Do you have any special skills?
8.   Tell me about yourself.
9.   Is there anything else I should know about you?
10. Are there any kinds of commercials you would not do?
11. Do you play any sports?
12. Do you have a job outside of school?
13. Why should I represent you?

Interviews can be challenging. You might need to practice this a couple of times to get it right. Get as many people as possible to interview you. Don't wait until you are at the agent's office to worry about what you are going to say.

A NOTE ON REJECTION:

No matter how much you practice, sometimes an agent just won't accept you. It could be they already have enough people your age. It could be they already have enough blondes (redheads, kids with braces, etc.) It could be that the agent doesn't think you are ready to go out on a real audition.

It could be that the agent is WRONG.

I have seen many young actors get rejected by various agents. Sometimes for dumb reasons. And those same young actors have gone on to have a wonderful commercial career. Sylvester Stallone was rejected by every agent in New York. And Chris Rock by every agent in Los Angeles. And look at them. One kid I coached got rejected by eleven different agents in one month. The twelfth agent accepted him and now he has done 23 commercials! Agents can be wrong.

If you are rejected, don't let it get you down. Just write another letter to another agent. Believe in yourself. And keep practicing your commercials. It never hurts to try. It just hurts to quit.

Pictures,

Résumés,

Work Permits

Your Pictures

I can't tell you enough how important good pictures are to your career. No wait, I'm sorry. Forget good pictures. You need GREAT pictures.

EXERCISE: REPEAT OUT LOUD TEN TIMES

"I will get great pictures. I will get great pictures!"

The exciting thing about interviewing Robert Kazandjian is his energy. I had heard, over and over again, how funny and positive he is. And when I finally met him for this interview, I found it to be absolutely true. But the most inspiring thing about Robert is that he takes that wonderful energy and uses it to get some of the best head-shots I have ever seen. Unlike a lot of photographers who shoot great pictures that look nothing like the kids, Robert brings out the best in each of his clients. So listen up. Here is his advice on how to have great pictures. (My questions are in italics, his answers follow.)

Hollywood 101 Insider:
Robert Kazandjian COMMERCIAL PHOTOGRAPHER, LOS ANGELES, CA

YOU ARE KNOWN IN LOS ANGELES AS "THE ONE ROLL KING". YOU SHOOT ONLY ONE ROLL AND YET, YOU GET ALL DIFFERENT LOOKS. WHAT ARE SOME DIFFERENT LOOKS A YOUNG ACTOR MIGHT USE IN A PHOTO? Commercially you want kids to look like they are having fun. Technically, on the commercial shot you want to show both ears, meaning show both sides of the face. Don't make it an angled shot where it is deceiving when they bring them in for a commercial audition. Theatrical shots depend on the look of the kid. If he is skinnier, then maybe a messy-hair bed-head look. You want to do it a little grungy, a little edgy. I might shoot it outside next to the dumpster. I want that energy. I don't want a mean look or an angry expression. I don't want them over-acting.

YEAH, I SEE THAT ALL THE TIME. It has to be natural. If you are going to do a pretty or handsome shot, it's all about the eyes. Not a blank stare. Teens always try that and I'll call them on it. If I see you staring at me waiting, anticipating, I'll make you do it again. I have them walk away, come back, and do it again. Or think of something. Sometimes I have them play a certain character, it depends on the age of the kid. And then, when they get into character, I shoot the shot.

WHAT ABOUT GIRLS? WHAT ARE THEIR DIFFERENT LOOKS? No different than guys except for hairstyle. Clothing has a lot to do with it, more so than guys. Girls always walk into my studio looking older than they are. Hairstyles can change that. We want kids to look their age. Or possibly even younger than their age, if they can pull that off. Pigtails sometimes will bring out the kid inside a kid. They feel giddy. You get a giddy vibe from them so it's a fun vibe. Jeans are the safest on the bottom. A couple of different blouses on top. But obviously nothing too busy.

OKAY SO YOU BROUGHT IT UP. WHAT IS BEST WHEN IT COMES TO CLOTHES? Texture is important, as in wool ribbed. Shirts that button up are also great. Things to avoid are logos on your shirt. The worst color to shoot is gray, as far as I'm concerned. Medium, muddy gray is exactly what it is going to come out as, not enough contrast. On kids, you want to stay a little brighter. Primary colors are always safe.

LET'S TALK ABOUT THE STYLE OF CLOTHES. You want a little love. For example, kids should wear what they would wear after school. Play clothes. Clean clothes, but casual. Don't go as far as sunday school clothes. In other words, don't dress up.

YEAH, I SEE THAT ALL THE TIME. KIDS REALLY DRESS UP IN THEIR PICTURES. MY RULE OF THUMB IS HOW MANY KIDS DO YOU SEE DRESSED UP ON TV? Very few. Yeah the GQ, high fashion look is not real big for a young actor. *WHAT ABOUT AN OLDER TEENAGER? DO THEY COME IN AND MAKE THE MISTAKE OF BEING TOO HIGH FASHION?* Yeah, especially the girls. Guys go the other way with ridiculously baggy clothes.

THAT LOOK IS SO PLAYED OUT. Yeah. Nobody looks good with baggy clothes. Girls are going the opposite direction. They are doing the Britney Spears thing. Tank tops and a sexy midriff.

AND THE HIP HUGGER JEANS. I try to avoid that look. Because agents want their kids to look young.

KIDS ARE TRYING TO GROW UP SO FAST. WHAT THEY DON'T UNDERSTAND IS THAT IN SHOW BUSINESS, THAT IS A BAD THING. PRODUCERS ARE ALWAYS GOING TO HIRE THE OLDER KID TO PLAY YOUNGER. SO IT IS STUPID FOR A KID TO DRESS SO MUCH OLDER. I SAY KIDS SHOULD ENJOY BEING THEIR AGE. ADULTHOOD WILL COME SOON ENOUGH. But getting a teenager to believe that is hard.

WHAT ARE THE BEST COLORS TO WEAR IN A COLOR PHOTO? You don't want to overpower the picture with color because it will take away from you. Purple is too strong of a color, so you don't want to use that. Go with soft colors. Every time I see someone go with bright yellow, all I see is the color and not the person. So go softer. Something that compliments you. And doesn't overpower you.

WHAT MAKES A GREAT BLACK AND WHITE PHOTO? Be careful of patterns. They can be too distracting. You can get away with flannel shirts because they have softer patterns. Tiny checks are horrible. Hawaiian shirts are fun but you have to be the right character to get away with it.

WHAT IS THE RIGHT CHARACTER? You know. Quirky. A fun guy. You have to live up to it. You can't be a shy person and think a shirt is going to make you exciting. Which brings me to a question you haven't asked me yet. What is the single ingredient that makes a great picture whether it is black and white or color?

Hey, who is doing the interviewing here? You give up?

YES. Movement. Remember pictures are flat. They are in 2-D. If you can add movement, it brings the photo to life. Adds personality.

WHAT SHOULD AN ACTOR EXPECT WHEN THEY COME TO ONE OF YOUR PHOTO SHOOTS? I tell them to bring their own music. Something that gets them in the mood for fun. And I love music, so I always talk about music with my clients. And we dance around. Laugh a lot. I like to joke around. It's important to get the mood right. If you do, then you just point the camera and shoot the fun.

ONCE THE PHOTO SHOOT IS OVER, WHAT HAPPENS? Well, I do something a little different from other photographers. Instead of a contact sheet, I make 4 x 6's. These are so much easier to look at and see the pictures.

I AGREE. MANY TIMES I'VE PICKED A HEADSHOT FROM A LITTLE TINY CONTACT SHEET. AND WHEN IT WAS BLOWN UP, IT DIDN'T LOOK THE SAME. That happens. So I pick my favorites and you take them to your agent or manager. Because they are the person who is going to be representing you. So their opinion is the most important.

MOST AGENTS WILL PICK ONE COMMERCIAL SHOT AND ONE THEATRICAL SHOT. THEN OF COURSE, YOU HAVE COPIES MADE. DO YOU HAVE A PREFERENCE BETWEEN LITHOGRAPHS OR REAL PHOTOS? I KNOW THAT LITHOS ARE A LOT CHEAPER. BUT I DON'T THINK THEY LOOK AS GOOD. That used to be the case. But today's lithos are much better. The quality is great.

WHEN DID THEY START IMPROVING THOSE? There is a new machine and what they do is scan the photo. Then they print out a template, it's a full 8x10 template and its all digital. The quality is just remarkable. WHAT ABOUT RETOUCHING? LET'S SAY A KID HAS A ZIT? I first try to cover it with a little makeup. But if I can't, then you can have it retouched. But scars you should leave. Because they are a part of you.

SO YOU USE MAKE UP? Rarely. Maybe a little translucent powder if they are shiny. Or on a kid if he is a really fair redhead and you can't see his eyebrows. Then you fill in a little bit. Otherwise, never.

HOW ABOUT PROPS? No, I feel like we are going back to the 80's. Everybody used props back then. But now that feels so dated. An exception might be a skater dude. That's if he is really a good skateboarder. Then I might put the board in a shot or two. It's the same with athletic wear. If you can play a sport, we'll shoot a couple of you in the jersey. Sometimes I might even put a little mud on your face. It gives the picture that edge.

ROBERT, THANKS FOR THE INTERVIEW. DO YOU HAVE ANY LAST WORDS OF ENCOURAGEMENT? Don't hold back on the fun. That's what makes a good picture.

Your Résumé

A résumé is a single sheet of paper stapled to the back of your picture. An actor's résumé is never more than a single sheet of paper! What is on a résumé?

The Actor's name

Contact number   Usually this is the agent's phone number

The Agent's Name

Hair color

Eye color

Height

Weight

Experience   This includes any plays, television or films that the actor has performed in.

Training   Listing of all classes taken. Include acting, dancing and any musical instruments you can play.

Special Skills   A list of everything that you can do. Include sports played, accents that you can imitate. Can you juggle or hackysax? Then put it down.

Here is an example of of a beginner's résumés. Yours should look something like this.

LULU BELL
310-555-5555

Height: 6' 9"   Weight: 43 lbs.
Hair color: Green   Eye color: Purple
Birthdate: 4/1/98

THEATRE

DON'T DRINK	Jewel	Elementary School
HALLOWEEN PLAY	Ghost	Elementary School
ST. PAUL'S PROMISE	Jezebel	1st Baptist Church

TRAINING
- Acting
      Drama Club   Bill Clinton Middle School - 2 yrs
- Dance
      Linda's School of Dance
            Jazz - One Year, Tap - Six months

SPECIAL SKILLS
Volleyball (Varsity), Basketball (Church League), Soccer (Goalie), Piano (Chopsticks), Swimming, Diving (Cannonballs), Impressions (Arnold Schwarzenegger, Hilary Duff, South Park), Accents (Southern: Texas & Tennessee), Burp On Cue

Your Work Permit

Now that you have your pictures and résumé finished, you need to think about a work permit. Have your parents/guardian read the following.

FOR PARENTS/GUARDIANS:

If your child is going to work in the entertainment industry, you must first research information on the state labor laws and education requirements. Usually your agent will give you the proper information. Each state has different requirements. Some states ban kids from working at all unless they receive a waiver. Others let the kids work if they receive permission from their school principal. Like I said, most agents will know what rules apply to you. But it never hurts to check yourself.

The best place to find this information is at: www.sag.org. They have a wonderful database which has information for all fifty states.

I recommend that you do this research before you get an agent. Many states require that you get a work permit. I have known a couple of young actors who signed with an agent on a Monday morning. Went to an audition on that Monday afternoon. And started working on Tuesday morning. Luckily, they already had their work permits. Don't let your child down. Get his/her work permit today.

The

Commercial

Audition

Your Commercial Audition

Okay, we're finally here. The moment you have been training for. You've been practicing commercials. You have an agent. You have great pictures with a resume stapled on the back. You have a work permit. Now you are ready for a job!

The phone rings. You rush to the phone.

You - Hello?

Agent - Hey babe. You got an audition! It's for Breath Mints. They loved your picture and they want to see you today at three pm.

You - Great!

Agent - Dress casual. You're part of a couple. And you're on a bench together. And one of you has bad breath. That's all I know. You got it, babe?

You - Sure. When do I get the lines?

Agent - They'll be at the audition. (She gives you the address.) Good luck. Oh and make sure you have fresh breath.

So you put on your best casual clothes and head to the audition. On the way there you do tongue twisters to get warmed up.

Step #1 - Get warmed up before you audition.

Then at 2:45 you arrive at the audition. (Always arrive at an audition fifteen to twenty minutes early. You'll need time to memorize your script.)

The Commercial Audition

Step #2 - Always arrive fifteen minutes early.

You look around. There are fifteen other actors/actresses your age all standing around waiting to audition. Oh no! The competition. Insecure thoughts come rushing into your head. What if I'm not good enough? What if I'm wasting my time? What if I go in there and totally mess up?

Then you remind yourself that you've been practicing your commercial technique for the last couple of months. And that you have a great agent who believes in you, and the casting director has already seen your picture and thinks you would be great for the job.

Step #3 - Get your confidence up.

Now, sign in. There should be a sign-in sheet around. Make sure you sign in for the right commercial. Sometimes in Los Angeles there are as many as ten commercials being cast in the same building. So make sure you sign up for Cat-A-Butter.

Step #4 - Sign in.

The next thing you do is see if there are any lines for the commercial. Not all commercials have lines. But if there are, you want to start working on them as soon as possible.

Step #5 - See if the commercial has lines.

You look around and find, right next to the sign-up sheet, a script for Cat-A-Butter.

The Commercial Audition

CAT-A-BUTTER

My cats are always bugging me. Meow! Meow! Meow! Meow! Meow! From the way they tell it, you would think they were always starving. Then I got new Cat-A-Butter from Whisko. It's a peanut butter for cats. One spoonful and their little mouths gets so gummed up that they can't meow all day. And they like the tuna peanut butter taste. So if you need some peace and quiet, try new Cat-A-Butter.

So you start memorizing. You want to be ready when they call your name.

Step #6 - Start memorizing your script, and start thinking about how you are going to perform it.

After about five minutes, you have it down. Your training is really working. You know exactly what you are going to do when you go in the audition room.

The casting director walks into the lobby and calls the names of a couple of actors sitting next to you. As they walk into the audition room, they each lay down a piece of paper. You glance at it. What is it? It looks like a cartoon strip (see Storyboard Graphic on pages 84-85).

This is called a storyboard. It shows the actor exactly what the director is looking for. Look at each frame. See how the action changes in each frame. After you memorize the commercial, memorize the storyboard.

Step #7 - Look at the storyboard and memorize the action.

A couple of minutes later, the casting director comes back into the lobby and calls your name. You walk into the audition room. She asks you to stand on a piece of tape on the floor facing the camera. You do. You are nervous and excited.

Then the casting director says, "SLATE".

Note: To "slate" is to say your name and your agent.

Example slates.

> *"How's it goin'? I'm Creegan Dow and I'm with Myrna Lieberman Management."*

> *"Hi. I'm Eli Montgomery and I'm with BBA."*

> *"Robby Azizi. William Morris."*

Always smile!

EXERCISE: - PRACTICE GIVING YOUR SLATE. BE FRIENDLY. GIVE IT YOUR OWN PERSONAL TOUCH. PRACTICE IT UNTIL YOU FEEL COMFORTABLE.

A good slate is very important. It is your first impression. You want to come across as professional and also fun to be with.

EXERCISE - DO YOUR SLATE IN FRONT OF A FRIEND.

Ask your friend what kind of impression you are making. Is it the answer you want? If not, change your slate until you appear both professional and a fun person to hang around.

Things <u>not</u> to do while slating.

- Scratch
- Chew gum
- Frown
- Mumble
- Pick your nose

After you slate, the casting director pairs you up with a partner and asks you to do the Breath Mint commercial.

You nail it! All those months of training have paid off.

"Great" she says. "But can you look at the camera less and at each other more?

_____

TAKING DIRECTION FROM A CASTING DIRECTOR:

There is only one way to take direction from casting directors. Do *exactly* what they tell you to do. It is that simple. The director of the commercial has told the casting director exactly what she wants. It is the casting director's job to find an actor who can give the director what he or she is looking for.

EXERCISE - MEMORIZE THE KAPLAN VIDEO COMMERCIAL.

KAPLAN'S CAMERA SHOP
(Teenager runs into his/her parent's bedroom, flips on the lights.)

Dad, Mom, wake up! I've finally decided what I want for graduation. Kaplan's new Mini Digital Video Camera. Mom! Wake up! It's got high resolution computer ready digital video and...Dad, you're snoring! Oh, and a 12x optical 48x digital zoom with image stabilization. Guys, get up! You can sleep later. Oh, and the best part is it's got a color LCD screen and view finder. (The parents don't move.) Okay, forget it. But don't blame me if you miss the half price sale at Kaplan's Camera Shop. (The parents jump out of bed and run for the door.) Hey guys! Wait up.

First practice performing it the way you think it should be. Then pretend that the casting director has given you one of the following *notes.*

        a. Every time you talk to your parents, yell.
        b. As you talk to your parents, run from one side of the bed to the other.
        c. Sit down on the line, "Okay, forget it."
        d. Trip as you come running into the room.
        e. Shake your dad to get him to stop snoring.

Keep performing the commercial until you have tried all of the *notes.*

How did you do? If you had trouble, keep working on it. An actor must be able to perform in hundreds of different ways. When you walk into an audition, you are never 100% sure what the casting director wants. So be flexible. Try any note they give you.

The Commercial Audition

EXERCISE - PICK ANY COMMERCIAL IN THIS BOOK. MEMORIZE IT. THEN MAKE A LIST OF TEN DIFFERENT WAYS YOU COULD PERFORM IT.

Examples:
- a. happy
- b. silly
- c. sad
- d. angry

After you have made your list, perform the commercial all ten ways.

———

Okay, back to the audition. You take the casting director's notes and do exactly what she said.

"Great." she says, "Thank you. Callbacks are tomorrow."

You leave the audition room happy. You survived your first audition. You not only survived it, you excelled. Aren't you glad I made you memorize all those commercials?

Now comes the worst part of being an actor: waiting for the phone to ring.

The casting director said the "callbacks will be tomorrow." A callback is another audition, but this time for the director. It is usually the last step before you get the job. Hopefully you will get a callback. But if you don't, don't worry about it. There is always another audition. And as anyone who has ever watched television knows, there is always another commercial.

NOTES ON CALLBACKS:

Here are a couple of things to remember when you get a callback:

1. Always wear the same clothes as you did on the original audition.

2. Do your commercial exactly the way you did it for the casting director.

3. Listen carefully to any notes the director gives you. He/She, and not the casting director, is the one who decides if you get the job or not.

Example: Commercial Storyboard

CAT-A-Butter

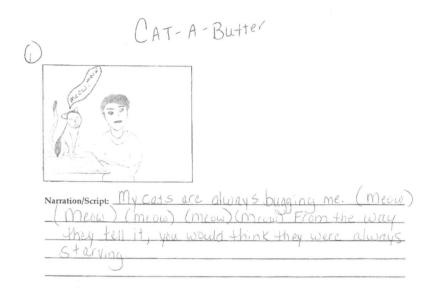

Narration/Script: My cats are always bugging me. (Meow) (Meow) (meow) (meow) (Meow) From the way they tell it, you would think they were always starving

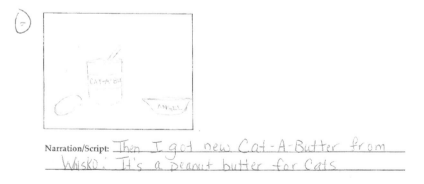

Narration/Script: Then I got new Cat-A-Butter from Whisko. It's a peanut butter for cats

Example: Commercial Storyboard

Narration/Script: One spoonful and their little mouths get so gummed up that they can't meow all day. And they like the tuna peanut butter taste.

Narration/Script: So, if you need some peace and quiet, try new Cat-A-Butter.

The Inside Scoop

Interviews with Five Hollywood 101 Insiders

What follows are five interviews with people who really know what's happening in the commercial industry. Read on and hear directly from agents what they are looking for in young actors. (My questions are in italics, their answers follow.)

Hollywood 101 Insider:
Cindy Osbrink THE OSBRINK AGENCY, LOS ANGELES, CA

HOW DO YOU FIND KIDS? Many different ways. My partner, Scot, travels around the country every other weekend scouting for new kids. Another way we find them is, of course, submissions. Parents send us a snapshot or a tape. And a little blurb about their personality. And lots of recommendations. Casting directors, directors, managers, etc. Sometimes, I'll meet with kids and they are not ready to work with me, but I'll sign them up with the commercial or print sections of my agency. To get them experience. I want to see how they do. And if they do well. I work with them theatrically.

HOW LONG HAVE YOU BEEN AN AGENT? Eleven years.

WHAT WAS YOUR BACKGROUND BEFORE YOU WERE AN AGENT? I was a stage mom. That's basically how I got started in the business.

WHEN YOU MEET A KID FOR THE FIRST TIME, WHAT DO YOU HAVE THEM DO? I have them come in and talk to me. I rarely have the kids read. I can tell just by them coming in and being themselves about the confidence they have. It's got to come from their hearts if they truly want to do this. I can see it in their eyes when I ask them, "Why do you want to be an actor?" And if they give me the right answer, they are in. *(She laughs.)*

(LAUGHING) I'M NOT GOING TO ASK YOU WHAT THE RIGHT ANSWER IS. I'm not telling you.

VERY FUNNY. NOW, WHAT CAN YOU TELL ME ABOUT THE KIDS' MARKET? WHAT IS HAPPENING IN LOS ANGELES? WHAT OPPORTUNITIES ARE THERE FOR KIDS? It has been amazing. Probably in the last couple of years, family oriented films, and teen films, have really taken off. We have producers literally coming to us, handing us scripts, and wanting us to attach our kids to the projects to help them get it made. That wasn't happening before. Most of my meetings lately are with producers. Because there is a big demand. Because of the success of films like <u>Holes</u> and all the family films that are a little bit edgy. Not the sugary sweet ones, but films where adults can like it, too. Same thing with teens. Films with Raven Symone or Lyndsay Lohan and all those guys. That's what's hot right now. And thank God. Kids are hot again.

HOW ABOUT IN THE COMMERCIAL MARKET? The strike hurt everyone in this town. But it is coming back. But in an unusual way. The producers are looking for those oddball kids. Right now, no one wants to see the pretty kids for commercials.

WHAT ADVICE DO YOU HAVE FOR YOUNG ACTORS WHO WANT TO GET STARTED? OTHER THAN STUDY EVERYTHING IN MY BOOKS, OF COURSE? I think the biggest thing is, it has to be their dream. They have to do it because they want to. Get in a commercial class. Get in a theatrical (film and television) class. Do a play. My biggest piece of advice is, follow your gut and you will never go wrong. Whether it's right or wrong, it's right for you. And that's when it's truly going to be believable. When it's right for you.

Hollywood 101 Insider:
Robin Dornbaum   JORDAN, GILL AND DORNBAUM AGENCY,
NEW YORK, NY

HOW DO YOU FIND KIDS? We find our kids through referrals and from parents mailing in snapshots of their children

WHEN THEY GET TO YOUR OFFICE, WHAT DO THEY ACTUALLY DO? Depends on the age of the child. If I am meeting three-to six-year-olds, I'm really looking at personality. The willingness to separate from their parents. I want a kid who is going to sit down, and when I say how are you, they proceed to tell me for the next ten minutes how they are. If I am interviewing kids seven-to-nine, I am really interested in their reading skills. So, I am going to talk to them to see their personality, but I am also going to give them copy to read. We do a cold read to see how good of a reader they are. Kids that are older, we are also going to give them copy to read for us.

WHAT DID YOU DO BEFORE YOU BECAME AN AGENT? Unlike most agents, I was not interested in being an actor. I think that most agents started out in the business as actors. I always had a passion for the entertainment business, and when I was in college, I did internships. The first internship I did was at a talent agency, and the second internship I did was at a casting office. I decided I liked the agent side instead of the casting side. I started working here at Jordan Talent, which is one of the oldest kids' agencies in New York City. I eventually ended up becoming partner, and my partner and I bought out Jordan. The Joe Jordan Agency has been around since the late 1950's, early 1960's.

WHAT IS THE MARKET LIKE IN NEW YORK CITY? I think that the New York market is so different from the Los Angeles market. The New York market is commercials. We have TV shows that shoot here but the majority of the real television work is still out in Los Angeles. It is not here. I think the feel of New York is much more casual than Los Angeles. My kids tend to think of this as just another after school activity. Usually, it is not the focus of their lives. It's like baseball, ballet, and then they have an audition. It's not like Los Angeles, where this is the focus of their career. I think that most of the kids in New York are doing commercials and voice-overs. Kids are doing <u>Saturday Night Live</u> and <u>The David Letterman Show</u>. They do whatever opportunities are here, but the opportunities don't compare to what they are in Los Angeles. Kids who exhaust the New York market and essentially want to succeed in the business, we send them out to Los Angeles. They go out for pilot season. Yes, you can book in New York, but the majority of pilots are booked out of Los Angeles. They don't want to pay to send kids out from New York.

WHAT ADVICE DO YOU HAVE FOR THE YOUNG ACTOR? My advice, more than anything, is to be the best kid YOU can be. I am interested in well-rounded kids; I'm not interested in kids that are focused on one thing. I want to know that you are skateboarding, dancing, and that you are doing other things. Essentially, I want the best *you* that you can be. That means going to school, being educated, and being well rounded in life. That's what we are looking for, much more than kids that are focused on just acting.

Hollywood 101 Insider:
Lily Liu LILY'S TALENT AGENCY, INC., CHICAGO, IL

HOW DO YOU FIND KIDS IN CHICAGO? We are listed in many creative directories; however, the best sources are referrals from my clients and talent that we work with. When potentials call our office for procedures and registration, we transfer them to our registration line. The registration line will ask them to send a couple pictures to us along with a cover letter including a resume, if any, any information about themselves that may be of interest to us, and a self-addressed stamped envelope for our response. Response time is generally two weeks.

HOW LONG HAVE YOU BEEN AN AGENT? Our agency celebrated our twenty-fourth anniversary in August, 2004. I have been an agent since 1980. Previous to that, I was a model and actress, so I know what it's like for actors and talent trying to get into the business. It can be intimidating. So, I try to explain the basics of the industry, as well as what they can expect from agencies. I also hold a degree in education and taught several years prior to having my agency. Therefore, I enjoy teaching and coaching talent to be professional. Also, I started my three daughters in the business. They became union franchised actors because of their success in landing union commercials. I pass on information on what is necessary to get cast.

WHAT DO KIDS DO WHEN THEY COME IN TO MEET YOU? If they are a child, we ask the parent to stay in the reception room while we walk the child to meet the agents. The agents are all very personable here, and they might ask the child if they have any siblings, what kind of food they like, if they have any pets, or anything they like to talk to us about. It only takes a few minutes for us to see if they are ready for the business. If a child is ready, we invite the parents to join the child and explain to them the necessary paperwork that needs to be turned into our office for registration. One would be the work permit. Children under sixteen need to have a work permit, so we hand them the letter of intent. We also give them our policies and guidelines sheet. The policy includes common sense information such as showing up on time, type of wardrobe necessary for various jobs, the casting process, etc. It's complete information listing our policy and guidelines. If they are comfortable with it, they then fill out the registration form if they have all the materials such as pictures or composites. With infants and toddlers, we don't request them to get composites. They can simply turn in pictures they have taken at home so long as they are in good focus and quality pictures. We suggest that the duplicate pictures are matted on an 8x10. Professional composites can be done at a later time. If a child can read, we ask them to read a child's copy of simple lines to check their skills.

WHAT IS THE MARKET LIKE IN CHICAGO? Chicago is still very much a commercial city. There are a lot of commercials being auditioned and shot in Chicago. We hand out several fliers and brochures of classes available in their age range. I suggest them to check the schools or classes out online, as well as calling them, and asking questions. We recommend perfecting their skills so that children have more success in getting cast.

WHAT ADVICE DO YOU HAVE FOR KIDS GETTING STARTED? I would tell kids to have confidence in themselves and to continue to develop their skills, and also don't have anybody get you down. It can be very competitive, so believe in yourself and do the best you can. Enhance your skills by taking classes, listen to your agent, and be well prepared for auditions.

Hollywood 101 Insider:
Peter Anthony PAGE PARKES CORP., DALLAS, TX

HOW DO YOU FIND KIDS IN DALLAS? We are the largest agency in the southwest. Because our agency does have such a great reputation, we get a lot of mail from all across the nation. We have an open call, which we conduct the last Thursday of the month. We have people coming in, whom we call "wannabes," that come in and hopefully, we can take some of these potentials, and develop them.

HOW LONG HAVE YOU BEEN AN AGENT? I've been in this industry for over twenty years. Fifteen years were spent in Los Angeles. I also worked on a series while I was an agent.

WHAT SERIES WERE YOU ON? I was on a reality TV program called <u>Sightings</u>, one of the first successful reality programs that paved the way for other reality programs today. I was on the forensic team.

YEAH, I REMEMBER "SIGHTINGS." IT WAS LOTS OF FUN. SO TELL ME, WHEN YOU MEET A KID FOR THE FIRST TIME, WHAT DO YOU HAVE THEM DO? It's not so much a matter of what we have them do; we've been in the business for such a long time, that we can tell as soon as they walk through the door. There is a certain energy that we respond to.

I KNOW WHAT YOU MEAN. IT'S THAT PASSION FOR ACTING. BESIDES COMMERCIALS, DO YOU DO THEATRICAL WORK? Exactly. Also television and feature films. So, back to your last question, the basic things we ask about is training. What have they done? Have they done school plays? Are they actually training right now? And what kind of training? Commercials? Improv? Things like that. If they are a model, we are looking for measurements and great features, photogenic features. And, of course, personality. That is the number one priority.

The Inside Scoop

EXCELLENT. TELL ME ABOUT THE KID'S MARKET IN DALLAS. WHAT EXACTLY IS THE MARKET THERE? We are actually a very strong secondary market. We are becoming one of the strongest markets in the nation because we have JCPenny, which is a huge client here, and Dillard's, so there is a lot of print in this town. Out of twelve months of the year, we stay busy ten months of the year. On the acting side of it, there is a lot of non-union; there are a lot of feature films that shoot in Austin, which is a three-hour drive away. We get the calls here, and we send the kids down to audition in Austin. Film season goes on all year-round here.

WHAT ADVICE DO YOU HAVE FOR YOUNG ACTORS THAT WANT TO GET INTO THE BUSINESS? Basically, if you really want to be an actor, you get in school plays and go out for community theatre. Perform as much as you can. Also, they should like to read. I mean in terms of education, a good actor has to be well read.

Hollywood 101 Insider:
Joy Pervis HOT SHOT KIDS/TEENS, ATLANTA, GA

HOW DO YOU FIND KIDS IN ATLANTA? I schedule only one open call per year. I never advertise; it is just word-of-mouth. My last call, I interviewed over 750 kids and teens. I am very selective about who I offer representation. I value quality of quantity. I only take kids that I know are marketable enough to book. Since I only have one open call per year, the rest of my kids come from referrals from casting directors, acting coaches, directors, producers, and talent searches.

HOW LONG HAVE YOU BEEN AN AGENT? I have been an agent for over eight years in Atlanta. Before I became an agent, I was in banking for fifteen years. I directed pageants for a while, then I opened a modeling school, and that led to my agency.

WHAT DO KIDS DO WHEN THEY COME IN TO MEET YOU? The initial impression is very important to me. They should be outgoing, personable, precocious (but controllable), outspoken, be able to follow directions, and have a vivid imagination! When a child reaches the age of seven, they have to be able to read very well. I spend the first few minutes interviewing the child, and then I hand them a script that they must be able to read with expression and good diction.

WHAT IS THE MARKET LIKE IN ATLANTA? Atlanta is a secondary market and is a great training ground for kids who wish to expand their career in the Los Angeles or New York markets. We have our share of commercial work, and there are a lot of film projects going on in the surrounding states, especially the Carolinas and Louisiana. I also work the LA Breakdowns and work with LA agent, Cindy Osbrink. She is an amazing agent! She gets my best kids.

The Inside Scoop

WHAT ADVICE DO YOU HAVE TO HELP KIDS GET INTO THE BUSINESS? Take every opportunity you can to get in front of the right people, find a great agent (one who believes in you), and get involved in a lot of different activities, not just acting. Being well rounded is so important in this business. The more activities you are involved in, the more marketable you are for your agent. You have to take the business seriously, but have fun with it as well. Just as with any other type of activity or sport, you should train on a regular basis to perfect your craft. If you are a gymnast, you would be at the gym practicing every week. If you are on a baseball team, you would be on the field practicing at least twice a week. The same should be if you are pursuing a career in acting. Find a great acting coach and be in class on a consistent basis. Some of my best referrals come from acting coaches.

This may be the end of the book, but for you it is just a beginning. I remember when I booked my first commercial. I was so excited about the chance to be on television. Throughout the fifty commercials and 100 plays I've performed in, that excitement has never left me. And I'm willing to bet, if you did all the exercises in this book, it will never leave you either.

Commercials are fun but they aren't the only way to be an actor. I want to encourage you to get involved with your local theaters. School plays and community theater are where most actors learn to act. There are very few things in life more fun than being on stage, in a great play, performing for hundreds, maybe even thousands, of people. If you need any help with an audition monologue, I have written a couple of books, MAGNIFICENT MONOLOGUES FOR KIDS, AND MAGNIF-ICENT MONOLOGUES FOR TEENS, (see last page), that will help you. And if you want to work on some television and film scenes, check out my books SENSATIONAL SCENES FOR KIDS and SENSATIONAL SCENES FOR TEENS.

Good luck!

Hey, wait a minute! Now that you're an actor, I should say what every actor hears on opening night.

Break-a-leg!

Chambers Stevens

Glossary

of Industry

Terms

Glossary of Industry Terms

Here are some words and phrases you need to know if you are going to be a professional actor. Take a second to read over them. Don't worry there's not going to be a test later.

AD LIB - To make up words not already in the script. If a director tells you to ad lib, what he means is ignore the script and say something your character would say. Also called improv.

AFTRA - Stands for the "American Federation of Television and Radio Artists". AFTRA is a union for actors.

AGENT - The person who gets you auditions. Then when you get the job, they take ten percent of your earnings.

AIR DATE - The date that your commercial shows on TV.

ATMOSPHERE - See "Extra".

AUDITION - The show biz word for "trying out" for a commercial.

BEAT - A moment. If the script says, "a beat," then that means take a small pause before you say your next line.

BLOCKING - Stage Movement. When the director gives you blocking, he is telling you where to stand and when to move.

BOOK - When you "book" a commercial that means that you have "won" the role.

BOOM - A microphone on a long pole.

BREAK-A-LEG - An actor's way of saying, "good luck".

CALLBACK - The second audition.

CASTING DIRECTOR - The person hired by the producer to find the right actors for the job.

Glossary of Industry Terms

CATTLE CALL - See "Open Call".

CLIENT - The person who has final say on a commercial. If it is a Pepsi commercial then "Pepsi" is the client.

CUE - Any signal that it is your turn to speak or move. If the director says "pick up your cues", he means that when the other actor stops talking, you start quicker.

CUE CARD - A piece of poster board with the actor's lines on it.

DIALOGUE - The lines you speak from your script.

DIRECTOR - The person who is in charge of the play or film. He or she instructs the actors, set designers, and every other part of the play or film.

EXTRA - A nonspeaking part. An extra appears in the background of the scene. Also called "Atmosphere".

FOCUS - Putting all your attention on one thing. If a director yells "focus", he/she means "listen up and concentrate".

GESTURE - The way you move your arms and hands.

HAND PROPS - Small things used by the actor. Like a purse or a baseball.

HEADSHOT - An 8" X 10" picture of an actor. Can be color or black/white.

IMPROVISATION - Acting without a script. Making it up as you go along.

LINES - The words you speak from the script. Learning your lines means to memorize the speeches your character has in the script.

OPEN CALL - An audition where you don't need an appointment. Also called a *Cattle-call* because open calls usually have tons of people waiting around like cattle.

Glossary of Industry Terms

PRINCIPAL - The main acting role with lines.

RESIDUAL - Money paid to an actor for the repeat showing of a commercial or TV show.

SAG - Stands for "Screen Actors Guild." SAG is a union for actors.

SECOND CALLBACK - Your third audition.

SIDES - Part of a script. When you audition, they give you sides to read from.

SLATE - What the casting director asks you to do at the beginning of a commercial audition. It means say your name, age, and what agency represents you.

STAND-IN - Extras who "stand in" for the lead actors while the crew focuses lights and the camera.

TAKE-A-BEAT - If the scripts says to "take a beat," it means to take a small moment before speaking.

TOP - The beginning. When the director says, "go from the top", he means start at the beginning.

UPGRADE - Being "upgraded" means when you are hired as an extra and the director gives you a line, thus making you a principal actor.

Index

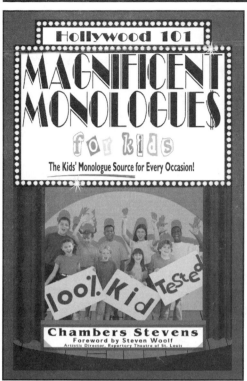

ISBN 1-883995-08-6

Magnificent Monologues for Kids

Includes...

• more than 50 *original* monologues, both dramatic and comedic, for teens

• straight talk about acting basics

and much more.

"Chambers helped me learn how to work in front of the camera. Before I met him, I was shy. Now, I'm starring in a TV show!"
—DEEDEE DAVIS, THE BERNIE MAC SHOW

"Educators will find Magnificent Monologues for Kids an excellent classroom resource for their speech and drama needs."
—DAVE MORENO, RECORDIST, BOSTON PUBLIC, ALLY MCBEAL, KING OF THE HILL

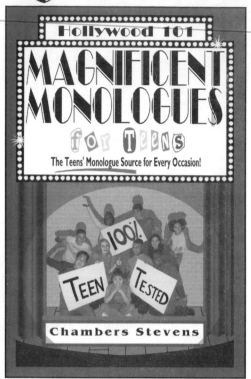

Magnificent Monologues for Teens

Includes...

• more than 50 *original* monologues, both dramatic and comedic, for boy and girls

• advice from industry veterans

and much more.

ISBN 1-883995-11-6

"Chambers helped me put that creative twist on my characters that go me the job."
— CLAYTON SNYDER, LIZZY MCGUIRE

"Chambers took the stage and the kids by storm. In less than one hour, their acting technique increased exponentially under Chambers' hands-on direction."
— WILLIAM EYERLY, PH.D.
PROGRAM DIRECTOR, GAINSVILLE ASSOC. FOR THE CREATIVE ARTS

Sensational Scenes for Kids

ISBN 1-883995-12-4

Includes...

• more than 30 *original* dramatic and comedic scenes for boy and girls

• scene-study exercises and much more.

"Being an actress is fun. But Chambers makes acting more than fun. He helps you be all that you can be."

—AMANDA DEARY
LILO AND STITCH

Sensational Scenes for Teens

ISBN 1-883995-10-8

Includes...

• more than 30 *original* dramatic and comedic scenes for teens

• advanced scene-study exercises and much more.

"Chambers is great! He draws out the best from the kids."

—MICHAEL ZODOROZNY
ANIMATOR, DARIA,
BEAVIS AND BUTTHEAD